THE TWO-WAY STREET

GUIDEPOSTS TO PEACEFUL SCHOOL DESEGREGATION

by SHELDON STOFF

DAVID-STEWART PUBLISHING COMPANY
3612 Washington Boulevard • Indianapolis, Indiana 46205

This work was originally conceived as a research study while I was on the staff of Cornell University. Dr. William Lowe provided much of the aid and friendship which made the completion of this study possible.

I would also like to thank Dr. Robin Williams, Jr., and Dr. Harold Cushman for their help.

Lastly, only Lorraine, my wife, can realize the depth of her contribution.

SHELDON STOFF
Queens College
of The City University
of New York
Flushing, New York

Library of Congress Catalog Card Number: 67–20804

FOREWORD

No one can reasonably deny the existence of a racial gap in the United States. And none realistically can hope to preserve it. An accumulation of shocking statistics bears out the sordid fact that Negro Americans have been disadvantaged through educational deprivation. Instead of debating causes, those who formulate and administer educational policies must find effective ways to improve the education of Negroes. Undeniably, this nation cannot afford to have a growing segment of its people unable to contend with the intellectual complexities of living and working in the late Twentieth Century. To improve the education of Negroes is, in a very real sense, to improve education for America.

So the American educational enterprise is being put to a test. How well it handles the issues related to the social revolution of the Negro American will determine, to a large extent, its ultimate effectiveness in contributing to constructive social change. Failure to mediate the issues of Negro education surely will have devastating effects on the system and the nation.

While the need for integration has been well established, the means to achieve it are less certain. Sheldon Stoff has provided a guidebook which should be of concrete, practical help to educators and members of boards of education as they face the crises of school integration. The author, after careful analysis of school desegregation efforts, has proposed a program for peaceful integration. Both students of, and practitioners in, the schools will profit from this book.

Equality of opportunity is a cornerstone of our national ethic. Yet there is nothing so unequal as the equal treatment of unequals. Negro children need to be educated with white children and, as important, white children must have the opportunity to work and play with Negro children. Learning to live in harmony and understanding with a different race must be part of the educational process.

Samuel Butler, over 300 years ago, wisely pointed out a truth appropriate to the issue of school desegregation when he said, "He that is convinced against his will is of the same opinion still." Integrating a school is a social as well as an administrative process. Thus, integration must take into account change in the dispositions of people, as much as change in the boundaries of schools.

Contemporary educators must be men of conviction and, at the same time, social engineers. Strife can so easily arise when men of conviction are insensitive to the attitudes and involvement of people in matters related to their schools. The challenge, then, is for educators and board members to develop programs which will enlist support for as well as acceptance of school integration.

The basic problems of improving education for Negro youth will not, however, be solved by integration alone. Important as it is, it is only a first step. Once schools are integrated, methods of instruction and content must be appraised and adjusted to help youngsters be all they are capable of being. However, until the first step is taken in integration, the succeeding developmental steps cannot be made.

School desegregation can be an occasion for educators to institute a number of practices that will enhance the total school program. For example, the in-service program begun for integration of faculties may be institutionalized to keep abreast continually of new educational developments. Integration may be the reason for a depth study of the school's program, identifying strengths and weaknesses. And the needs of integration may provide the stimulus for the addition of specialists in reading, audio-visual aids, or curriculum. The occasion of school desegregation, then, is an opportunity as much as a challenge.

Nothing could be more harmful to the education profession in the long run than to have educators standing idly by while others mandate accommodations to the racial revolution. Who knows better how to meet the issues related to education than educators? Thus, educators must lead and not follow their communities in improving the education of all the children of all the people.

David W. Beggs, III
Bloomington, Indiana
May, 1967

PREFACE

In 1954 the Supreme Court of the United States ordered the desegregation of public schools with "all deliberate speed." In the Brown decision, Chief Justice Warren delivered the opinion of a unanimous court. He stated that "to separate them [school children] from others of similar age and qualifications solely because of their race generates a feeling of inferiority as to their status in the community that may affect their hearts and minds in a way unlikely ever to be undone."

I do not intend to present, in this study, a moral or social discussion of the ethics of this decision. It is the law of the land, supported by a majority of the population, and, in fact, most of the people contacted in this study believe that desegregation is inevitable. Apparently, most people are ready to challenge any concept of racism.

In the summer of 1963 I was fortunate enough to be able to devote ten weeks to teacher-training work for the Peace Corps. We were engaged in training a group of people who were to be secondary teachers in Sierre Leone. Even while we were training a group of dedicated people for service in Africa, the racial issue in the United States flared. One morning, in reviewing the *Daily Mail*, a Sierre Leonian paper available for our group, this distressing headline appeared:

APC [All People's Congress] **DEPLORES INCREASING RACIAL STRIFE IN U.S.**

If one wanted to write subjectively about the moral, logical, and political aspects of the desegregation issue, his supply of arguments and counter-arguments would be endless. We have been deluged with that kind of writing. I do, however, adhere to these biases: Nonviolence in desegregation is morally preferable to violence; nonviolence as a way of social change is more logical than violence; nonviolence as a way of social interaction is more politic than violence.

Nonviolence is usually not an accident. It prevails because certain community settings are conducive to nonviolence. For those interested in maintaining the dignity of each person, in making school transition as peaceful as possible, this volume is intended as a guide to action. From school board members to the clergy, paths of responsibility can now be spelled out and statistically supported. This book, then, is written as a guide to thinking about appropriate ways to meet the consequences of the social revolution of the American Negro.

The information presented here is based on contacts with 189 communities in the Southern and border states that experienced public school desegregation from September 1960 to October 1963. Contacts have also been maintained with more recently desegregated school systems, and the insights gained from them have been included. There is little reason for those intimately concerned with the schools in one community to fail to learn from the experiences of friends of the schools in other communities.

Chapter I gives historical perspective to the desegregation movement. Chapter II discusses the mechanics of the statistical analysis. Those not interested in the statistical background could easily jump from Chapter I to Chapter III, where specific influences on the desegregation climate are spelled out.

The tables in the Appendix comprise the statistical background. The most pertinent information from them has been extracted and presented in the study where appropriate. Appendix A contains some of the more pertinent desegregation plans and comments forwarded to me.

CONTENTS

I

A History of the Main Trends in School Desegregation in the United States

A Theory of Social Change

A study of past school desegregations has convinced me that where racial desegregation of public schools has been brought about in a nonviolent manner, either positive action has been taken by persons in leadership positions or specific conditions in the transition communities have precluded the outcropping of violence. In other words, specific factors, events, or deeds are associated with nonviolent school desegregation. This research seeks the isolation and description of these factors.

I have supported a theory of social change that agrees with Professor Kenneth Clark's: "Desired changes in the behavior of individuals and groups can be brought about by a change in the social situation in which they are required to function."[1] He believed that skilled persons, with accurate information, could act so as to vary some community situations, utilize and recognize others, and institute a community situational set which would support nonviolent school desegregation.

A prior claim, now supported by this research, stated that social change in school desegregation could be brought about in a less disruptive, nonviolent manner when there is—

1. open communication between groups, in good faith working toward common goals
2. firm leadership for non-violent desegregation to serve as a unifying force in this direction

[1] Kenneth B. Clark, "Desegregation: An Appraisal of the Evidence," *Journal of Social Issues,* 1953, No. 4, p. 72.

3. allegiance to the American Creed, upheld and explained
4. an understanding attitude when implementing change and respect for the dignity of the opposition.

Early Efforts for Negro Education

The early history of the education of the Negro American is characterized by a large zero. Education was denied Negroes by white men. In part, this denial was based on the fear that educated Negroes would not, in all probability, accept their position as slaves. The very structure of slavery would be threatened, which would in turn affect the white man's economic life. As pointed out by Knight and Hall, the denial of education for the Negro was often supported by legal statute. South Carolina imposed a fine of "one hundred pounds current money" on anyone who would "teach, or cause any slave or slaves to be taught, to write, or shall use or employ any slave as a scribe in any manner of writing whatsoever."

This attitude was maintained, with notable exceptions, for years to come. The General Assembly of Virginia, in 1831, prohibited the teaching of slaves, free Negroes, or Mulattoes to read or write. Before and during this time there were also state laws prohibiting the education of Negroes or prohibiting their attendance in public schools in Georgia and Louisiana. Similar prohibitions were enacted in Alabama (1832), South Carolina (1834), Washington, D.C. (1834), Missouri (1847), and Texas (1866). The usual punishment for teaching Negroes was a fine, imprisonment, or lashes; however, a Methodist minister who had taught Negroes was pulled from his pulpit on a Sunday morning by an angry mob and subjected to abuses at the town water pump.

Some of the notable exceptions to this attitude were the early attempts at Negro education which were inspired by religious groups.

> An early catechizing school was founded in New York City at Trinity Church in 1704. Instruction was given by Elia Neau regularly until 1712, when blame for a local slave uprising was attributed by some masters to Neau's work.[2]

At this point, he was forced to cease his work. Efforts at educating the Negro were continued by Catholics, and a strong effort was launched by the Quakers. In no Northern states were laws passed against teaching Negroes even though such education was often feared. Still the educational level of Negroes in the North was well below that of their white brethren.

---

[2] Virgil A. Clift, *et al.* (eds.), *Negro Education in America* (New York: Harper and Brothers, 1962), p. 34.

Education Permitted

Following the close of the Civil War, efforts were increased to provide greater educational opportunities for the Negro. The new attempts were usually made within the context of white supremacy and were not aimed at equality of opportunity.

> It must be remembered, nevertheless, that violent opposition abated as years passed. Though barriers of caste were to be raised in the New South (1877-1913) as Southern white rule was destroyed, the idea of support for the academic education of the Negro began to receive sympathetic acceptance. By the turn of the century, some communities of the South were giving limited financial support to a segregated Negro education that was controlled by whites, unequally supported, and devoted almost exclusively to elementary or industrial education.[3]

During this period of time increased efforts for the education of the Negro were made in New York, Michigan, Massachusetts, Connecticut, Alabama, Iowa, Louisiana, South Carolina, New Jersey, Pennsylvania, and California. Efforts to provide for segregated education were instituted in Nevada, Georgia, Mississippi, North Carolina, Texas, Virginia, Indiana, and Ohio.[4]

Education and Desegregation

Many Northerners are surprised to discover that the "separate but equal" doctrine was apparently born in the North rather than in the South. It is interesting that a key court case arose in a stronghold of the abolitionists, Boston, Massachusetts.

Many communities in Massachusetts had abolished racially segregated schools prior to 1849. Then Benjamin Roberts, a Boston Negro, tried to enroll his five-year-old daughter in a white elementary school. Five white schools were closer to his home than the nearest Negro school. His bid was rejected. His attorney contended that the school board had no authority to maintain segregation and "brand a whole race with the stigma of inferiority."[5] He further contended that schools should foster understanding, and that separation of the races would lead to bias and ignorance.

---

[3] Clift, p. 39.

[4] William Brickman and Stanley Lehrer (eds.), *The Countdown on Segregated Education* (New York: Society For The Advancement of Education, 1960), p. 154.

[5] Milton R. Konvitz, *A Century of Civil Rights* (New York: Columbia University Press, 1961), p. 126.

Massachusetts State Chief Justice Shaw delivered the unanimous opinion of the court and held that the school board did have the power to enforce segregation. He further held that the legal authority and power in education was "exclusively with them [the board]."[6]

The ruling stated—

> The "great principle" that "all persons without distinction of age or sex, birth or color, origin or condition are equal before the law," when applied "to the actual and various conditions of persons in society," does not lead to the conclusion that all persons "are legally clothed with the same civil and political powers." Laws may be enacted that are "adapted" to the "respective relations and conditions" of people or classes of people.[7]

This reasoning was later applied to other court cases which strongly supported the "separate but equal" doctrine (in New York, Arkansas, Missouri, Louisiana, and West Virginia). It constituted a precedent for upholding segregated education. And his view was in the fabric of the thinking of white Americans' attitudes in regard to Negroes in all phases of their life, including education.

As the efforts to educate the Negro increased, support for education arose from several quarters. The churches continued their previous efforts. Among them were the American Missionary Association, the Friends Association for Aid to Freedmen, the Presbyterian Church, the Methodist Church, and the Baptist and Episcopal Churches. Wealthy Northerners provided financial aid. Among the leaders were the Peabody fund with a contribution of $3,500,000, the Slater fund with a contribution of $2,000,000, the Carnegie fund with a contribution of $10,000,000, the Rockefeller fund with a contribution in excess of $1,000,000, and the Rosenwald and Jeanes funds. These grants aided school construction, scholarships, endowments, teacher training, and industrial development.[8]

The Southern states also made efforts in this direction, but, before 1900, many of the efforts were completely inadequate. "The Southern states were spending an average of $4.92 per year on a white child in 1900 and $2.71 on a Negro child."[9]

Under the influence of Samuel C. Armstrong and Booker T. Washington the Negroes were apparently willing to accept segregation in their schools, churches, and industry as long as improvements and a sense of equality could

---

[6] *Ibid.*, p. 127.
[7] *Ibid.*, p. 127.
[8] Clift, pp. 40-42.
[9] *Ibid.*, p. 44.

be provided in these areas. To do otherwise in the South, at that time, was unsafe and unrealistic.

The Supreme Court case of *Plessy* v. *Ferguson* in 1896 upholding racial segregation in transportation seemed to settle the issue for a period of time. The question of concern to the court was the reasonableness of the regulation, not the issue of properness of segregation *per se*. The dissenting opinion by Justice Harlan criticized this ruling which seemingly branded Negroes an inferior class of citizens. Here is an excerpt from his decision:

> Americans boast of the freedom enjoyed by our people above all other people. But it is difficult to reconcile that boast with a state of the law which, practically, puts the brand of servitude and degradation upon a large class of our fellow citizens, our equals before the law. . . .
>
> Our Constitution is color blind, and neither knows nor tolerates classes among citizens.[10]

The *Plessy* v. *Ferguson* decision enabled states, such as Kentucky, to prohibit mixed schools with the sanction of the U.S. Supreme Court. There was no doubt of Kentucky's position.

> It shall be unlawful for any white person to attend any schools or institutions where negroes are received as pupils or receive instruction, and it shall be unlawful for any negro or colored person to attend any school or institution where white persons are received as pupils or receive instruction. Any person so offending shall be fined fifty dollars for each day he attends such institution or school.[11]

Though the promise was "separate but equal," inequality in financial support prevented the Negroes from achieving this equality. The U.S. Supreme Court even held constitutional a Georgia school segregation law providing state funds for white schools although there were no provisions made for Negro schools.

Even with these shortcomings, there was some improvement of Negro schools. But equality was never achieved. In recent years some Southern states have spent from 21 percent to 94 percent as much on their Negro students as on their white students.[12]

During later years there was still a strong carry-over from previous days.

---

[10] U.S. Supreme Court Justice Harlan, *Plessy* v. *Ferguson* (163 U.S. 537, 1896).

[11] Acts of the General Assembly of the Commonwealth of Kentucky (1904), pp. 181, 182.

[12] U.S. Dept. of Health, Education and Welfare, Office of Education, *Statistics of State School Systems, Organization Staff, Pupils and Finances 1953-1957* (Washington, D.C.: U.S. Government Printing Office, 1954), Ch. 2, p. 114, Table 48.

There are many recorded reports of threats to white teachers of Negro students, such as the note quoted below:

> Mr. Banks we thought we would give you a chance to save yourself one of the worst scourings that a man ever got and you can do so by reading this note and acting upon its contents. You have set up a nigger school in the settlement which we will not allow you to teach if you were a full blooded negro we would have nothing to say but a white skin negro is a little more than we can stand you can dismiss the school immediately or prepar yourself to travail we will give you a chance to save yourself and you had better move instanter.[13]

The Beginning of Desegregation

The desegregation attempt, lost by Benjamin Roberts, continued with greater success in the twentieth century. In 1923, in a school district where the Negroes outnumbered the whites and where the Negro school was of inferior quality to the white school, an Oklahoma court ruled that inequality existed.

In 1936 Donald Murray, a Negro graduate of Amherst College, applied for admission to the University of Maryland Law School. There was no Negro law school in the state. The Court of Appeals ordered his admission to the school. The desegregation battle was in full swing and moving in a positive direction. The long battle for human equality was moving ahead.

Two years later the U.S. Supreme Court ruled that Missouri must admit a Negro applicant to the University of Missouri Law School because of the absence of a Negro law school. They also ruled that opportunity and payment of fees in out-of-state schools did not constitute equal opportunity. This was a second significant step toward desegregated education.

Other breakthroughs followed in West Virginia University, the archdiocese of St. Louis, the University of Oklahoma Law School, the University of Delaware, the University of Arkansas, and in Indiana. These steps were specific in application and did not seriously threaten the "separate but equal" doctrine. The right of the Negro to acquire an equal education where none had previously existed was now fairly secure.

Apparently, the most resounding defeat to segregation in education, to that date, was registered by the U.S. Supreme Court in *Sweatt* v. *Painter*. In this decision the very heart of the *Plessy* v. *Ferguson* decision was put to question.

---

[13] *State Journal* (Alabama, 1875); given in E. Knight and Clifton Hall, *Readings in American Educational History* (New York: Appleton-Century-Crofts, Inc., 1951), p. 679.

Whether the University of Texas Law School is compared with the original or the new law school for Negroes, we cannot find substantial equality in the educational opportunities offered white and Negro law students by the State. In terms of number of faculty, variety of courses and opportunity for specialization, size of the student body, scope of the library, availability of law review and similar activities, the University of Texas Law School is superior. What is more important, the University of Texas Law School possesses to a far greater degree those qualities which are incapable of objective measurement but which make for greatness in a law school. Such qualities, to name but a few, include reputation of the faculty, experience of the administration, position and influence of the alumni, standing in the community, traditions and prestige.[14]

The Big Decision

The most direct and far-reaching victory in the battle against segregated education was achieved in 1954. It was the culmination of a long series of legal attacks waged against segregated education. The decision attacked the heart of the segregation issue and opposed the previous "separate but equal" doctrine. It was an opinion supported by social science research. Chief Justice Warren delivered a unanimous court opinion:

> We must look instead to the effect of segregation itself on public education. . . .
>
> Today, education is perhaps the most important function of state and local governments. . . . It is the very foundation of good citizenship. . . . Such an opportunity where the state has undertaken to provide it, is a right which must be made available to all on equal terms. . . . To separate them [children in grade and high schools] from others of similar age and qualifications solely because of their race generates a feeling of inferiority as to their status in the community that may effect their hearts and minds in a way unlikely ever to be undone. . . .
>
> We conclude that in the field of public education the doctrine of "separate but equal" has no place. Separate educational facilities are inherently unequal.[15]

This ruling and subsequent rulings by the Supreme Court indicated a "reasonable but steady course" for school desegregation. The end was in sight, the goal inevitable; a slow but steady public school desegregation was now a legal reality. As Clift, *et al.* phrased it—

> The initial decision and subsequent rulings in the years following indicate that, although a satisfactory readjustment of the school systems in America might take a long period of time, eventually the democratic processes in education would be extended to all areas of the United States.[16]

---

[14] *Sweatt* v. *Painter* (339 U.S. 629, 1950).
[15] *Brown* v. *Board of Education* (347 U.S. 483, 1954).
[16] Clift, p. 204.

Where Desegregation Stands Today

Desegregation in the Southern and border states has been steady. It has increased far more rapidly in the border states than in the Southern states. The following tables, reproduced from the *Southern School News,* illustrate this progress.

TABLE 1

SCHOOL DESEGREGATION, 1954-64

Grades Kindergarten-12 in 17 Southern and Border States and D. C.

		School Districts			Enrollment		In Desegregated Districts		Negroes in Schools with Whites	
		Total	With Negroes & Whites	Deseg.	White	Negro	White	Negro	No.	%+
1954-55	South	4,355	3,337	3	6,105,378	2,315,062	NA	NA	23	.001
	Border.....	6,214	907	156	2,438,611	323,752	NA	NA	NA	NA
	Region	10,569	4,244	159	8,543,989	2,638,814	NA	NA	NA	NA
1955-56	South	4,204	2,909	78	6,349,790	2,417,798	419,670*	21,299*	2,782	.115
	Border.....	5,654	912	329	2,470,787	324,539	NA	251,247	NA	NA
	Region	9,858	3,821	407	8,820,577	2,742,337	NA	272,546	NA	NA
1956-57	South	4,055	2,885	110	6,478,796	2,437,893	524,539	26,285	3,514	.144
	Border.....	5,642	810	573	2,645,015	360,408	1,323,405**	298,989	106,878++	NA
	Region	9,697	3,695	683	9,123,811	2,798,301	1,847,944**	325,274	110,392++	NA
1957-58	South	3,047	2,090	137	6,770,710	2,538,554	638,842	51,949	3,829	.151
	Border.....	5,467	813	621	2,656,865	385,397	1,313,919**	325,337	127,677++	NA
	Region	8,514	2,903	758	9,427,575	2,923,951	1,952,761**	377,286	131,506++	NA
1958-59	South	3,227	2,095	144	6,938,867	2,609,447	752,357	85,494	3,456	.132
	Border.....	4,647	780	596	2,711,653	398,971	1,509,156**	361,528	142,352++	NA
	Region	7,874	2,875	740	9,650,520	3,008,418	2,261,513**	447,022	145,808++	NA
1959-60	South	3,164	2,095	153	7,225,977	2,636,320	1,000,997	148,391	4,216	.160
	Border.....	3,852	756	602	2,777,822	420,943	1,550,024**	372,022	191,114	45.4
	Region	7,016	2,851	755	10,003,799	3,057,263	2,551,021**	520,413	195,330	6.4
1960-61	South	3,115	2,095	172	7,358,920	2,660,438	1,449,040	305,167	4,308	.162
	Border.....	3,548	744	611	2,824,798	436,429	1,657,090**	400,996	212,895	49.0
	Region	6,663	2,839	783	10,183,718	3,096,867	3,106,130**	706,163	217,203	7.0
1961-62	South	3,063	2,265	214	7,549,251	2,792,186	1,922,545	486,698	6,725	.241
	Border.....	3,307	782	698	2,856,477	457,402	1,661,282**	431,419	240,226	52.5
	Region	6,370	3,047	912	10,405,728	3,249,588	3,583,827**	918,117	246,951	7.6
1962-63	South	3,038	2,279	277	7,739,629	2,842,315	2,742,728	644,764	12,868	.453
	Border.....	3,160	775	702	2,915,921	486,016	2,023,419	451,870	251,797	51.8
	Region	6,198	3,054	979	10,655,550	3,328,331	4,766,147	1,096,634	264,665	8.0
1963-64	South	2,994	2,256	443	7,919,371	2,894,563	3,544,181	985,690	34,110	1.18
	Border.....	3,127	772	717	3,002,046	514,125	1,858,134**	496,756	281,731	54.8
	Region	6,121	3,028	1,160	10,921,417	3,408,688	5,402,315**	1,482,446	315,841	9.3

*** -- Estimated**
**** - Missouri not included**
+ -- Negroes in schools with whites compared to total Negro enrollment
++ - Missouri and West Virginia not included
NA -- Not Available

TABLE 2

SCHOOL DESEGREGATION, 1966-67

	School Districts				Enrollment		Negroes in Schools with Whites	
		With	In HEW Compliance					
	Total	Negroes & Whites	Yes	No	White	Negro	No	%
Alabama	118	118	66	52	571,200	273,800	12,000**	4.4
Arkansas	406*	222	391	12	337,920++	119,817++	18,100**	15.1
Florida	67	67	65	2	967,721	289,871	64,574	22.3
Georgia	195*	189	151	45	776,281**	388,140**	34,300**	8.8
Louisiana	67	67	46	21	502,870	317,785	10,697	3.4
Mississippi	148*	148	94	55	309,413++	293,831++	7,258	2.5
North Carolina	169	169	156	13	828,583++	355,107+	54,600**	15.4
South Carolina	107	107	89	18	377,077	265,400	14,853	5.6
Tennessee	151*	133	148	4	693,143	184,511	52,691	28.6
Texas	1,314*	862	1,306	6	2,185,000**	355,000+	159,400**	44.9
Virginia	135	127	127	8	760,758+	243,553+	61,500**	25.3
SOUTH	2,877	2,209	2,639	236	8,309,966	3,088,815	489,973	15.0
Delaware	49*	44	50	0	89,438	21,333	21,333	100.0
District of Columbia	1	1	1	0	13,369	133,275	114,976	86.3
Kentucky	200	167	200	0	613,919	185,884	121,359	90.1
Maryland	24	23	24	0	605,043	185,884	121,359	65.3
Missouri	878*	212	689	0	852,770+	130,000**	101,100	77.7
Oklahoma	988*	310	995	0	536,800**	61,600**	31,300**	50.8
West Virginia	55	44	55	0	403,246+	22,800**	21,300**	93.4
BORDER	2,195	801	2,014	0	3,114,585	615,432	465,939	75.7
REGION	5,072	3,010	4,653	236	1,424,551	3,704,247	955,912	25.8

* The sum of districts in and not in HEW compliance does not equal the state total because the Office of Education reports a different number of districts from that given by the State Department of Education.
** USOE estimate + Unofficial estimate ++ 1965-66

The main problem was the achievement of an orderly and nonviolent school desegregation. The nature of the Supreme Court decision allowed for sufficient time in achieving this desegregation. The nature of the communities involved indicated that a certain amount of violence would accompany its inception.

Resistance to school desegregation mounted after the Supreme Court order. Klan activity increased. No one doubts that "violence likely will continue to plague efforts to desegregate schools. . . ." It is the incidence of that violence that I hope to help mitigate by presenting this study.

II

The Mechanics of the Statistical Findings of the School Desegregation Situation

The Setting

All communities in the Southern and border states, identified in the various news media and the *Southern School News* as communities which had undergone initial school desegregation in the period of time from September 1960 to October 1963, were considered in this study.

Contacts within these communities, either of NAACP[1] members or chief school administrators, and further investigation through the aforementioned news media, indicated that 26 of the communities originally identified had apparently desegregated prior to September 1960. Information from these communities indicated that, in some of them, school desegregation was not *de facto*. In others, it was of such a limited and unidentified nature (so few Negro students were involved that most people were unaware of the event) that the news media were reporting them as initial desegregations. With these considerations and qualifications, all originally identified communities have been retained in this study.

The population considered for investigation consisted of 324 Southern and border communities. This was believed to be the entire population which was desegregating within the time and geographic area under consideration.

I selected, for testing, those variables which appeared to be significant in the attainment of nonviolent public school desegregation. They included nearly all stated assumptions and specific recommendations I could locate.

[1] The National Association for the Advancement of Colored People.

The variables were found in such works as *Schools in Transition, Action Patterns in School Desegregation,* and in current news media.[2]

Pilot Studies

In order to test the validity of the information furnished from field contacts, two communities were selected for a pilot study. Sufficient information had been previously obtained from these two communities, New Orleans and Atlanta, to provide this study with a standard by which to judge accuracy from the field. The variables were as follows: nonviolence, the state of desegregation, community size, percent of Negroes in the community, percent of all minority groups, percent of the population foreign born, Negro median income, percent of Negro students initially desegregated, police in plain clothes, Negroes on the police force, actions of law enforcement agencies, the desegregated state of restaurants and recreational facilities, the position of the newspapers, the position of local organizations, the possible economic advantages to desegregation, past Negro voting, the position of white community members, the state of desegregation of nearby schools, the role of the school administrator on opening day, the role of the school board, the state of desegregation of the teachers' organizations, the role of the white students, the behavior of Negro students, and the activity of individuals in opposition.

When there was no uniformity of response, usually one of the respondents had answered, "I don't know." The most serious inaccuracy occurred in response to the question regarding the "median income—all families," where respondents indicated a level of income ranging from $2,000 to $4,999 and the Census Bureau indicated an actual level of $5,758. It is of interest to note that respondents replied uniformly, although their judgments were low.

No attempt was made to establish a consensus or compromise of responses. If differing viewpoints on evaluation of events, as opposed to description of events, existed, I believed these viewpoints should be presented separately.

The Questionnaire, the Population, the Respondents

The variables upon which information was obtained were these (Appendix B):

---

[2] Robin M. Williams, Jr., and Margaret W. Ryan (eds.), *Schools in Transition* (Chapel Hill: The University of North Carolina Press, 1954); Herbert Wey and John Corey, *Action Patterns in School Desegregation* (Bloomington, Indiana: Phi Delta Kappa, Inc., 1959).

1. the state of school desegregation
2. the year of school desegregation
3. the method of school desegregation (voluntary vs. court-ordered)
4. the occurrence of personal violence
5. the occurrence of property damage
6. community size
7. percent of Negroes in the community
8. the total percent of all minority groups
9. the percent of the population foreign born
10. the median income for all families of the local community
11. the median income for all nonwhite families of the local community
12. the median school years completed for the male population of the community
13. the median school years completed for the nonwhite male population of the community
14. the percent of professional, technical, and kindred workers in the total population
15. the percent of sound dwelling units in the community, with all plumbing facilities
16. the employment level of the male, nonwhite population
17. the employment level of the male, white population
18. the percent of the desegregated student body which is Negro the first year of school desegregation
19. the total percent of the Negro school population attending desegregated schools
20. police on duty in plain clothes at the time of school desegregation
21. negroes on the police force at the time of school desegregation
22. action by the law enforcement agencies at the time of school desegregation
23. the racial composition of local labor unions
24. Negro demonstrations prior to school desegregation
25. the desegregation of restaurants
26. the desegregation of community transportation facilities
27. the desegregation of parks, pools, theaters, and sporting arenas
28. a functioning two-party political system
29. the role of the newspapers
30. the role of television stations
31. the role of local organizations
32. the role of the civic administration

33. efforts to gain support of lower class white groups
34. efforts made to make the white community aware of possible economic advantages of school desegregation
35. Negro voting
36. efforts made to alleviate possible fears of venereal disease
37. residential segregation
38. support by respected white (nonpolitical) community leaders
39. the rate of school desegregation
40. the state of segregation at local parochial schools
41. the nearness of desegregated public schools
42. the comparable quality of local Negro and white schools
43. the role of the chief school administrator in the development of a school desegregation plan
44. the role of the chief school administrator in support of a school desegregation plan
45. the role of the chief school administrator on the initial day of school desegregation
46. the role of the school board in supporting school desegregation
47. the state of desegregation of interschool sports, music programs, student council meetings
48. the state of desegregation of the faculty
49. the role of the white faculty in the preparation of white students for nonviolent school desegregation
50. the role of local labor unions
51. job security for all school personnel
52. a school desegregation office
53. a workshop in intergroup relations for the white faculty
54. the state of desegregation of the teachers' organizations
55. consultation by the local school administration with previously desegregated schools
56. the perceived academic ability of the Negro and white students
57. sufficient classroom space for school desegregation
58. practices of state educational agencies
59. two or more school districts desegregating at the same time
60. maintenance of desegregated school districts without regard to race
61. permissive vs. required individual student desegregation
62. the academic standing of Negro students in the initial school desegregation
63. the state of desegregation of school transportation facilities

64. the role of the white students
65. the instruction of Negro students in proper behavior
66. the role of the parents of white students
67. the expected maintenance of academic standards after school desegregation
68. the state of desegregation of the communities' churches
69. the role of the white churches in support of public school desegregation
70. cooperation by intergroup organizations, the school board, and the civic administration
71. an advisory committee to help plan school desegregation procedures
72. a general community interracial committee
73. the distribution to community leaders of pamphlets favorable to school desegregation
74. opposition to school desegregation by local individuals
75. opposition to school desegregation by outside individuals
76. opposition to school desegregation by the governor
77. opposition to school desegregation by local organizations
78. opposition to school desegregation by the local civic administration
79. opposition to school desegregation by outside organizations
80. opposition to school desegregation by the state education department

In December 1963 and January 1964 questionnaires were forwarded to contacts in all 324 communities. Due to insufficient addresses or errors in the listings of the communities in the news media, I could not make contacts in 19 cases. These letters were returned by the post office. Thus, there were a total of 305 communities actually contacted and considered as the population for this study. A total of 365 mailings were sent to NAACP and school administrator contacts in these 305 communities. In 60 randomly selected communities two contacts were made, providing a greater likelihood of obtaining at least one reply. Reminders were forwarded to all contacts not replying in ten days. One hundred eighty-nine replies were received covering 179 communities. Thus, a total of 62 percent of the communities responded. The breakdown of replies goes as follows:

1. *NAACP members*—
   contacted: 130
   initial replies: 22
   reminded replies: 22
   total replies: 44 percent replying: 34
2. *Chief school administrators*—
   contacted: 235
   initial replies: 104

reminded replies: 41
total replies: 145 percent replying: 62

3. *Total responses*—
total mailings: 365
initial replies: 126
reminded replies: 63
total replies: 189 percent replying: 52

percent of communities replying: 62

Table 3, on pages 16-25, provides a complete presentation of all data collected from items 1-74 of the questionnaire. This information is utilized in the statistical analyses which follow.

Responses to items 1-74 of the questionnaire are presented in Table 3. Included in these responses were ten (nonviolent to person or property) communities where responses were obtained from both NAACP and school administration contacts. No attempt was made to synthesize or abstract this data in Table 3 because a full presentation of data was desired.

All correspondence received from the field was coded on the basis of *initial reply* vs. *reminded reply* in an attempt to discern any tendencies in the group not replying immediately. An analysis of *Initial Replies* vs. *Reminded Replies* in columns 8 and 10, physical and property violence, gave the following results:

Physical Violence—Column 8

Violence		*Nonviolence*		
initial replies:	3	initial replies:	10	percent of violent communities: 3.0
reminded replies:	3	reminded replies:	60	percent of violent communities: 5.0

Property Damage—Column 10

Violence		*Nonviolence*		
initial replies:	4	initial replies:	100	percent of violent communities: 4.0
reminded replies:	2	reminded replies:	61	percent of violent communities: 3.3

A "t" test of column 8, where maximum difference existed, revealed that there was no statistically significant difference between the sample which replied immediately and the sample which replied after reminders were sent. A degree of reliability in the population was therefore assumed.

The author attempted no statistical analysis of those ten communities where there was a duplication of NAACP-chief school administrator re-

TABLE 3

DATA FROM 189 QUESTIONNAIRES CONCERNING SCHOOL DESEGREGATION

Variables						No Answer, Don't Know or Miscellaneous
1. Desegregation			yes: 167		no: 12	?: 10
2. Year of Desegregation			before 1960: 26		1960-64: 143	?: 20
violent			: 2		: 5	
nonviolent			: 24		: 138	
3. Voluntary vs Court Ordered			voluntary: 123		court ordered: 52	?: 14
violent			: 0		: 6	?: 1
nonviolent			: 123		: 46	?: 13
4. Personal Violence			yes: 6		no: 161	?: 22
5. Property Damage A total of 7 different communities experienced either personal or property violence.			yes: 6		no: 161	?: 22
6. Community Size (V)	1-1,499= 0	1,500-9,499= 1	9,500-19,999= 0	20,000-49,999= 1	50,000 or more = 5	?: 0
nonviolent	" =21	" =39	" =35	" =23	" =46	?: 18
7. Percent of Negroes in the Community (V)	0-9%= 0	10-24%= 2	25-49%= 5	50-74%= 0	75% or more = 0	?: 0
nonviolent	" =53	" =62	" =40	" = 3	" = 1	? or misc: 23
8. Total Percent of All Minority Groups (V)	0-9%= 0	10-24%= 1	25-49%= 4	50-74%= 1	75% or more = 0	?: 1
nonviolent	" =37	" =59	" =51	" =10	" = 1	?: 24

TABLE 3 (Continued)

Variables								No Answer, Don't Know or Miscellaneous
9. Percent of the Population Foreign Born (V) nonviolent		0-2%= 2 " =118		3-6%= 0 " =14	7-10%=0 " =2	10% or over=0 " =4		?: 5 ?: 43
10. Median Income All Families (V) nonviolent	-$1,499=0 " =1	1,500-2,499= 0 " =12	2,500-3,499= 0 " =20	3,500-4,499= 2 " =18	4,500-5,499= 0 " =16	5,500-6,500=0 " =5	6,500-over = 0 " = 4	?: 5 ?: 60
11. Median Income, non-white (V) nonviolent	-$1,499=0 " =4	1,500-2,499= 1 " =48	2,500-3,499= 0 " =37	3,500-4,499=0 " =9	4,500-5,499=0 " = 5	5,500-6,500=0 " =1	6,500 or over = 0 " = 1	?: 6 ?: 67
12. Median School Years Completed of Male (V) nonviolent	-5=0 "=1	5-7= 0 " =15		8-10= 1 " =72	11-12= 0 " =31	12+=0 " =4		?: 6 ?: 60
13. Median School Years Completed, Nonwhite Males (V) nonviolent	-5= 0 "=12	5-7= 2 " =58		8-10= 0 " =38	11-12= 0 " =10	12+=0 " =1		?: 5 ?: 63
14. Percent of Professional, Technical and Kindred Workers (V) nonviolent	-1%=1 " =9	2-4%= 0 " =32	5-9%= 0 " =21	10-14%= 1 " =18	15-20%= 1 " =14	20%+= 1 " =19		?: 3 ?: 70
15. Percent of Dwellings, Sound (V) nonviolent	-35%= 0 " =15	35-44%= 1 " =15	45-64%= 2 " =13	65-74%= 0 " =18	75-84%= 1 " =25	85%+= 0 " =35		?: 3 ?: 57
16. Employment Level, Male, Nonwhite (V) nonviolent	below average = 3 " =40		average = 2 " =76		above average = 0 " =23			?: 2 ?: 43

TABLE 3 (Continued)

Variables							No Answer, Don't Know or Miscellaneous
17. Employment Level, Male, White (V) nonviolent			below average = 0 " =10	average = 4 " =92		above average = 0 " =37	?: 3 ?: 43
18. Percent of Desegregated School Body, Negro (V) nonviolent	0%=0 " =1	-1%= 7 " =97	1-9%= 0 " =50	10-24%=0 " =7	25-50%= 0 " =50	50+%= 0 " = 0	?: 0 ?: 25
19. Total Percent of Negro School Population in Desegregated Schools (V) nonviolent	0%=0 " =1	-1%= 7 " =99	1-9%= 0 " =37	10-24%= 0 " =10	25=50%= 0 " = 7	50+%= 0 " = 5	?: 0 ?: 23
20. Police in Plain Clothes (V) nonviolent		not apply = 0 " =24	no = 1 " =119	? = 1 "=10	yes = 5 " =30		
21. Negores on the Police Force (V) nonviolent			no = 1 " =105	? = 0 "=29	yes = 6 =48		
22. Positive Action by Law Enforcement Agencies (V) nonviolent		not apply = 1 " =43	no = 3 " =44	? = 0 "=16	yes = 3 " =62		
23. Desegregated Labor Unions (V) nonviolent		no unions = 2 " =48	no = 4 " =49	? = 1 " =45	yes = 0 " =30		

TABLE 3 (Continued)

Variables						
24. Negro Demonstrations (V) nonviolent		no = 3 " = 121		? = 0 " = 26		yes = 4 " = 35
25. School Desegregation before Desegregation of Restaurants (V) nonviolent	no = 1 " = 27		? = 0 " = 24		same time = 0 " = 2	yes = 6 " = 125
26. School Desegregation before Desegregation of Transportation (V) nonviolent	no public transport. = 0 " =41		no = 4 " =77	? = 1 " =10	same time = 0 " = 2	yes = 1 " = 53
27. Desegregated Recreational Facilities (V) nonviolent	no = 7 " = 116			? = 0 " = 36		yes = 0 " = 30
28. A Two-Party Political System (V) nonviolent	no = 3 " = 63			? = 0 " = 24		yes = 4 " = 86
29. Newspapers Support Desegregation (V) nonviolent	no commitment = 4 " = 50	no = 1 " = 28		? = 0 " = 34	yes = 1 " = 78	split = 1 " = 1
30. T. V. Supports Desegregation (V) nonviolent	no. commitment = 3 " = 34	no = 1 " = 20		? = 1 " = 87	yes = 2 " = 41	split = 0 " = 0
31. Organizations for Desegregation (V) nonviolent	no = 4 " = 112			? = 1 " = 36		yes = 2 " = 34
32. Civic Administration Supporting Desegregation (V) nonviolent	no = 4 " = 99			? = 1 " = 37		yes = 2 " = 46

TABLE 3 (Continued)

Variables					
33. Efforts to Gain Lower Class Support (V) nonviolent	no = 5 " = 104		? = 2 " = 33		yes = 0 " = 45
34. Possible Economic Advantages (V) nonviolent	no = 5 " = 98		? = 1 " = 33		yes = 1 " = 51
35. Desegregation Before Negro Voting (V) nonviolent	no = 6 " = 144		? = 0 " = 22		yes = 1 " = 10
36. Attempts to Alleviate Fears of V.D. (V) nonviolent	no = 6 " = 115		? = 1 " = 50		yes = 0 " = 17
37. Breaks in Residential Segregation (V) nonviolent	no = 5 " = 109		? = 1 " = 31		yes = 1 " = 42
38. Respected White (nonpolitical) Support (V) nonviolent	0 = 0 " = 18	1-3 = 0 " = 8	4-9 = 1 " = 6	10+ = 3 " = 68	? - 3 " - 82
39. Rate of School Desegregation (V) nonviolent	gradual = 6 " = 102		? = 0 " = 26	all-at-once = 1 " = 54	
40. Public School Desegregation before Parochial Schools (V) nonviolent	no = 2 " = 38	no parochial schools = 1 " = 59	yes = 3 " = 71	same time = 1 " = 1	? - 0 " - 13
41. Nearness of Desegregated Schools (V) nonviolent	0-14 miles = 0 " = 26	15-50 = 2 " = 73	none within 50 miles = 5 " = 55		? - 0 " - 28

TABLE 3 (Continued)

Variables				
42. Equality of Negro and White Schools (V) nonviolent	no negro schools = 0 '' = 20	comparable = 2 '' = 95	not equal = 5 '' = 64	? - 0 '' - 3
43. School Administration A Leader in Desegregation Plan Development (V) nonviolent	no = 4 '' = 57		? = 0 '' = 29	yes = 3 '' = 96
44. School Administration Actively Support Desegregation Plan (V) nonviolent	no = 4 '' = 59		? = 0 '' = 28	yes = 3 '' = 95
45. School Administrator's Support on Opening Day (V) nonviolent	no = 2 '' = 26		? = 1 '' = 33	yes = 4 '' = 123
46. School Board's Support of Desegregation (V) nonviolent	no = 3 '' = 46		? = 0 '' = 31	yes = 4 '' = 105
47. School Desegregation before Inter-school Activities (V) nonviolent	no = 1 '' = 56		? = 0 '' = 30	yes = 6 '' = 96
48. A Desegregated Faculty (V) nonviolent	no = 6 '' =146	same time = 0 '' = 5	yes = 1 '' = 7	? = 0 '' = 26
49. White Faculty Prepared White Students (V) nonviolent	no = 4 '' = 18		? = 1 '' = 41	yes = 2 '' = 123
50. Labor Unions Support Desegregation (V) nonviolent	no unions = 1 '' = 58	no = 4 ''= 52	? = 2 '' = 62	yes = 0 '' = 10

TABLE 3 (Continued)

Variables				
51. Job Security for all (V)	not apply = 0	no = 4	? = 2	yes = 1
nonviolent	" = 28	" = 87	" = 29	" = 38
52. A School Desegregation Office (V)		no = 5	? = 0	yes = 2
nonviolent		" = 138	" = 24	" = 20
53. A Faculty Intergroup Workshop (V)		no = 5	? = 1	yes = 1
nonviolent		" = 111	" = 45	" = 26
54. Desegregated Teacher's Organization (V)		no = 7	? = 0	yes = 0
nonviolent		" = 110	" = 26	" = 46
55. Consultation with Desegregated School Personnel (V)		no = 2	? = 3	yes = 2
nonviolent		" = 51	" = 45	" = 86
56. Equal Negro Academic Ability (V)		no = 5	? = 2	yes = 0
nonviolent		" = 105	" = 57	" = 20
57. Sufficient Classroom Space (V)		no = 0	? = 1	yes = 6
nonviolent		" = 24	" = 23	" = 135
58. State Education Agencies Favorable to Desegregation (V)		no = 5	? = 1	yes = 1
nonviolent		" = 39	" = 44	" = 99
59. Other Schools Desegregated at Same Time (V)		no = 7	? = 0	yes = 0
nonviolent		" = 101	" = 33	" = 48
60. Desegregated School Districts without Regard to Race (V)		no = 5	? = 1	yes = 1
nonviolent		" = 92	" = 34	" = 56

TABLE 3 (Continued)

Variables							
61. Individual Desegregation (V)		permissive = 4	required = 2	both at different levels = 0			? = 1
nonviolent		" = 99	" = 49	" = 6			" = 4
62. Only Top Negro Students in Initial Desegregation (V)			no = 5		? = 1		yes = 1
nonviolent			" = 138		" = 27		" = 17
63. School Transportation (V)		not desegregated = 4	desegregated same time = 1	prior deseg. = 0	no school transp. = 0		? = 2
nonviolent		" = 48	" = 64	" = 19	" = 19		" = 49
64. White Students Support Desegregation (V)			no = 5		? = 2		yes = 0
nonviolent			" = 103		" = 48		" = 31
65. Negro Students Instructed in Proper Behavior (V)			no = 1		? = 2		yes = 4
nonviolent			" = 43		" = 49		" = 89
66. Some White Parents Support Desegregation (V)			no = 4		? = 2		yes = 1
nonviolent			" = 88		" = 39		" = 55
67. Expected Maintenance of Academic Standards (V)			no = 3		? = 2		yes = 2
nonviolent			" = 61		" = 47		" = 74
68. Desegregated Churches (V)			no = 4		? = 0		yes = 3
nonviolent			" = 101		" = 42		" = 39
69. White Churches Role in Desegregation (V)	Opp. = 1	no stand = 3	no church = 0	outside church sup. = 0	sup. = 2	Split = 0	? = 1
nonviolent	" = 2	" = 65	" = 1	" = 1	" = 65	" = 1	" = 47

TABLE 3 (Continued)

Variables						
70. Cooperation-Intergroup Organization, School Board and Civic Administration (V)	organ of school bd = 3	org. and civic adm. = 0	no coop = 3	unsuc. attempts = 0	organ. of school bd. and civic admin. = 0	? = 1
nonviolent	" = 55	" = 11	" = 103	" = 9	" = 9	" = 46
71. Advisory Committee for School Desegregation (V)		no = 3		? = 2		yes = 2
nonviolent		" = 106		" = 13		" = 40
72. Interracial Committee for General Problems (V)		no = 4		? = 0	it broke down = 1	yes = 2
nonviolent		" = 109		" = 8	" = 0	" = 42
73. Pamphlets to Community Leaders (V)		no = 5		? = 2		yes = 0
nonviolent		" = 133		" = 13		" = 13
74. Opposition by Local Individuals (V)	none opposed = 1			? = 2	active opposition = 4	
nonviolent	" = 106			" = 26	" = 27	
75. Opposition by Outside Individuals (V)	none opposed = 4			? = 1	outside indi. opposed = 2	
nonviolent	" = 133			" = 14	" = 12	
76. Opposition by the Governor (V)	no opposition = 3			? = 1	governor opposed = 3	
nonviolent	" = 140			" = 14	" = 4	
77. Opposition by Local Organizations (V)	no opposition = 1		? = 2		local org. opposed = 4	
nonviolent	" = 125		" = 22		" = 10	

TABLE 3 (Continued)

Variables			
78. Opposition by the Local Civic Administration (V)	no opposition = 5	? = 2	civic adm. opposed = 0
nonviolent	" = 138	" = 16	" = 3
79. Opposition by Outside Organizations (V)	no opposition = 3	? = 1	outside org. opposed = 3
nonviolent	" = 133	" = 19	" = 7
80. Opposition by the State Educational Department (V)	no opposition = 4	? = 1	state education dept. opposed = 2
nonviolent	" = 136	" = 22	" = 3

sponse. There were no differences in columns 8 and 10, those concerning violence, in these replies. The small number of duplicated replies and a number of "I don't know," responses by the NAACP contacts indicated that no meaningful correlations could be undertaken.

The Matched Communities Analysis

The next job was the establishment of the statistically significant differences in variables between those communities which desegregated in a violent way compared to those communities which desegregated their schools in a non-violent manner. Each of the seven violent communities was matched with three nonviolent communities. The nonviolent communities were selected on the basis of a maximum number of matched variables with the violent communities.

These groups were then compared on the basis of five separate constants. Matched comparisons were considered and computed independently for each of the five constants in order to assure maximum matching of variables between communities in each case. A total of 101 communities were thus represented.

The constants used are listed below:

1. urbanism
2. percent of Negroes in the population
3. median school years completed for the nonwhite male population
4. community income, all families
5. action by the local civic administration

The summary of these variables in the violent vs. nonviolent communities in a matched communities analysis is presented in Table 4. It indicates variables which were significantly different in the two groups under consideration. (See Appendix C for the complete table.) It established the factors which were significantly different in the violent vs. the nonviolent communities. The difference in social setting of the violent and nonviolent communities could now be clearly seen.

Related Variables of the Matched Communities Analysis

Those variables identified as significantly different under two or more constants were as follows (I arbitrarily selected only those variables for de-

TABLE 4

SUMMARY--THE MATCHED COMMUNITIES COMPARISON

riables/Constants	Urban-ity	Percent Negroes in the Population	Family Income	Years of Negro Education	Civic Admin.
Desegregation?	-	-	-	-	-
Year of Desegregation	-	-	-	-	-
Voluntary vs Court Ordered	-	-	-	**	*
Physical Violence	**	**	**	**	**
Property Damage	**	**	**	**	**
Community Size	X	*	*	-	-
Percent of Negroes in Community	-	X	-	*	**
Percent of all Minority Groups	-	-	-	-	*
Percent of Population Foreign Born	-	-	-	-	-
Median Income All Families	-	-	X	-	-
Median Income Non-White Families	-	-	-	-	-
Median School Years Completed, Males	-	-	-	-	-
Median School Years Completed, Non-White Males	-	-	-	X	-
Percent of Professional, Technical, Kindred Workers	-	-	-	-	-
Percent Dwellings, Sound	-	-	-	-	*
Employment, Male, Non-White	-	-	-	*	*
Employment, Male, White	-	-	-	-	-
Percent Desegregated Student Body Negro	-	-	-	*	-
Percent Negro School Population Desegregated	-	-	-	-	*
Police in Plain Clothes	-	*	**	**	**
Negroes on Police Force	-	-	**	**	**
Positive Action by Law Enforcement Agencies	*	-	-	-	-
Desegregation of Labor Unions	-	*	-	*	-
Negro Demonstrations	-	-	-	-	*
Desegregation of Restaurants	-	-	-	-	-
Desegregated Community Transportation	-	-	-	-	-
Desegregated Recreational Facilities	-	-	-	-	-
A 2-party Political System	-	-	-	-	-
Position of Newspapers	-	-	-	-	-
Position of TV Stations	-	-	-	-	-
Position of Local Organizations	-	-	-	-	-
Position of Civic Administrators	-	-	-	-	X
Efforts to Gain L. C. Support	-	-	-	-	-
Possible Economic Advantages	-	-	-	-	-
Negro Voting	-	-	-	-	-
Fears of V. D.	-	-	-	-	-
Residential Segregation	-	-	-	-	-
Respected White Support	-	-	-	-	-

TABLE 4 (cont.)

Variables/Constants	Urbanity	Percent Negroes in the Population	Family Income	Years of Negro Education	Civi Adm
39. Rate of Desegregation	-	-	-	-	-
40. Desegregated Parochial Schools	-	-	-	-	-
41. Nearby Desegregated Public Schools	-	-	*	*	*
42. Equality of Negro and White Schools	**	*	-	-	-
43. School Administration of the Desegregated Plan Development	-	-	-	-	-
44. School Administration Support for Desegregated Plan	-	-	-	-	-
45. School Administration Support on Opening Day	-	-	-	-	-
46. School Board Support of Desegregated Plan	-	-	-	-	-
47. Desegregated Interschool Activity	-	-	-	-	-
48. Desegregated Faculty	-	-	-	-	-
49. White Faculty Prepared White Students	-	**	*	**	**
50. Labor Union Support	-	-	-	-	-
51. Job Security for All	-	-	-	-	-
52. A School Desegregation Office	-	-	-	**	-
53. A White Faculty Workshop	-	-	-	-	-
54. Desegregated Teachers' Organization	-	-	-	-	-
55. Consultation with Desegregated School	-	-	-	-	*
56. Equal Negro Academic Ability	-	-	-	-	-
57. Sufficient Classroom Space	-	-	-	-	-
58. Role of State Educational Agencies	-	*	**	-	-
59. Schools Desegregated at Same Time	*	-	*	-	-
60. Desegregated School Districts Without Regard to Race	-	-	-	-	-
61. Permissive Desegregation	-	-	*	-	-
62. Top Negro Student in Initial Desegregation	-	-	-	*	-
63. Desegregated School Transportation	-	-	*	-	*
64. Role of White Students	-	-	-	-	-
65. Negro Students Instrumental in Behavior	-	-	-	-	-
66. White Parental Support	-	-	-	-	-
67. Maintenance of Academic Standards	-	-	-	-	-
68. Desegregated Churches	-	-	-	-	-
69. Position of Church Leaders	-	-	-	-	-
70. Cooperation by Intergroup Organizations, School Board, and Civic Administration	-	-	-	-	-
71. Advisory Committee for School Desegregation	-	-	-	-	-

TABLE 4 (cont.)

Variables/Constants	Urbanity	Percent Negroes in the Population	Family Income	Years of Negro Education	Civic Admin.
72. Community Interracial Committee	-	-	-	-	*
73. Pamphlets for Community Leaders	-	-	**	-	-
74. Opposition by Local Individuals	-	-	*	**	*
75. Opposition by Outside Individuals	-	-	-	-	-
76. Opposition by Governor	-	**	**	**	**
77. Opposition by Local Organization	*	**	**	**	**
78. Opposition by Civic Administration	-	-	-	-	-
79. Opposition by Outside Organization	-	-	**	**	**
80. Opposition by State Educational Department	-	-	*	*	-

** Significant at the .01 level
* Significant at the .05 level

scription which were significantly different under two or more constants as a further indication of replicability of the variables involved.):

1. voluntary vs. court ordered desegregation
2. community size
3. employment of males, nonwhite
4. police on duty in plain clothes at the time of school desegregation
5. Negroes on the police force at the time of school desegregation
6. the racial composition of labor unions
7. the nearness of previously desegregated schools
8. the comparable quality of Negro-white segregated schools
9. the white faculty preparing the white students for nonviolent school desegregation
10. the policies of the state educational agencies
11. two or more nearby schools desegregated at the same time
12. desegregation of school transportation
13. opposition of local individuals to school desegregation
14. opposition of the governor of the state to school desegregation
15. opposition of local organizations to school desegregation
16. opposition of outside organizations to school desegregation
17. opposition of the state education department to school desegregation

The variables now listed to indicate how they were associated significantly with nonviolent school desegregation were—

1. voluntary school desegregation (as opposed to the requiring of a court order)
2. smallness of communities (smaller ones experienced less violence)
3. high employment of the Negro male population
4. no police on duty in plain clothes at the time of school desegregation
5. no Negroes on the police force at the time of school desegregation
6. desegregated labor unions
7. nearness of previously desegregated schools
8. comparable Negro-white segregated schools
9. the white faculty prepared white students for nonviolent school desegregation
10. favorable action by the state educational agencies
11. two or more nearby schools desegregated at the same time
12. a desegregated school transportation system (before or at the same time as the school desegregation)
13. a lack of opposition to school desegregation by local individuals
14. a lack of opposition to school desegregation by the governor
15. a lack of opposition to school desegregation by local organizations
16. a lack of opposition to school desegregation by outside organizations
17. a lack of opposition by the state education department

Respondents' Evaluation of Persons, Groups, or Events Making a Significant Difference in Community School Desegregation

(as indicated on pages 12-13 of the questionnaire, obtained by analyzing rank, order, and the descriptive preferences of those replying) See tables 5, 6, and 7, which follow on pages 31 and 32.

Related Variables, Complete Listing

The combined listing of variables favorable to peaceful school desegregation (statistically significant in the Matched Communities Study and also noted by 10 percent or more of both groups as being favorable to nonviolent school desegregation) are now considered *pertinent variables*. The identification of these variables, and hence a favorable community set for nonviolence was the first order of this research study. The variables isolated are these:

TABLE 5

PERSONS, GROUPS OR EVENTS FAVORABLE TO NON-VIOLENT SCHOOL DESEGREGATION
(noted in at least 5% of the replies, by group)

	School Adminis-trators (102 contacts supplying this information	NAACP Members (38 contacts supplying this information)
	Percent	
Court Action	-	18
Favorable Action by School Administrators	50	24
Community Good Will	11	-
Favorable Action by the NAACP	5	61
Favorable Action by Interracial Groups	8	16
Favorable Newspaper Coverage	15	10
Lack of Publicity	14	-
Favorable Action by Community Leaders	11	18
Favorable Action by Civic Groups and Clubs	6	13
Favorable Action by the Civic Administration	17	5
Favorable Action by the School Board	55	37
The Economic Savings of School Desegregation	10	-
Favorable Action by the PTA	12	-
Favorable Action by the White Faculty	27	5
Favorable Action by Church Leaders	22	34
Favorable Action by the White Student Body	10	-
Favorable Action by Northern Business Managers or Military Personnel	-	5
Few Negroes in the Community	6	-
Favorable Action by the Principal of the Negro School	5	5
Fear of Bad Community Image	-	5
Favorable Action by Negro Citizens Groups	-	5
Favorable Television Coverage	5	5
Favorable Police Action	5	8
Favorable Action by the Lay Advisory Committee	6	5
An Unavoidable Procession	6	-

TABLE 6

PERSONS, GROUPS OR EVENTS CONTRIBUTING TO VIOLENT SCHOOL DESEGREGATION
(as indicated on pages 12-13 in the questionnaire, obtained by analyzing rank order and descriptive preferences of those replying)

	School Administrators	NAACP Members
	Percent	
Negro Demonstrations	1	-
Desire of Segregationists to Maintain Segregation	-	6
Unfavorable Action by Civic Groups and Clubs	1	-
Outside Agitators	1	3
Unfavorable Police Action	1	-
Unfavorable Action by the Governor	1	3
Unfavorable Action by the State Department of Education	-	3

TABLE 7

PERSONS, GROUPS, OR EVENTS NOTED BY TEN PERCENT OR MORE OF BOTH GROUPS AS BEING FAVORABLE TO NONVIOLENT SCHOOL DESEGREGATION

	School Administrators	NAACP Members
	Percent	
Favorable Action by School Administrators	50	24
Favorable News Coverage	15	10
Favorable Action by Community Leaders	11	18
Favorable Action by the School Board	55	37
Favorable Action by Church Leaders	22	34

1. voluntary school desegregations (as opposed to the requiring of a court order)
2. smaller communities
3. high employment of the Negro male population
4. no police on duty in plain clothes at the time of school desegregation
5. no Negroes on the police force at the time of school desegregation
6. desegregated labor unions
7. nearness of previously desegregated schools
8. comparable Negro-white segregated schools
9. preparation of white students by white faculty for nonviolent school desegregation

(Favorable action by school administrators, indicated pertinent by group evaluation, are defined in this study in the next two variables.)

10. chief school administrator led in development of a school desegregation plan
11. chief school administrator supported school desegregation plan
12. favorable action by state educational agencies
13. favorable action by the school board
14. two or more nearby schools desegregating at the same time
15. a desegregated school transportation system (before or at the same time as the school)
16. favorable newspaper coverage
17. favorable action by community leaders
18. favorable action by church leaders
19. a lack of opposition to school desegregation by local individuals
20. a lack of opposition to school desegregation by the governor
21. a lack of opposition by local organizations to school desegregation
22. a lack of opposition by outside organizations to school desegregation
23. a lack of opposition by the state education department

Correlation Matrix and Factor Analysis

The previous listing of the twenty-three pertinent variables is deemed to be important in itself. But it provides no cohesive plan or a framework for describing or examining the factors. Therefore, a factor analysis of these variables was undertaken which might hopefully indicate social constructs, infer relationships, aid in a grouped, orderly description of variables, and help clarify what had occurred.

For the computation of the factor analysis, a 23 x 23 correlation matrix was utilized, followed by an orthogonal analysis utilizing a program already available at the Cornell Computing Center. The resulting correlation matrix, together with the total 80 x 80 correlation matrix, with data significant at the .01 level, is presented in Appendix D.

To those not familiar with statistics this would mean that if chance was the explainer of these events, there was only a one percent likelihood of getting the results obtained.

The pertinent variables contained in the 23 x 23 correlation matrix were factor analyzed by the Cornell Computing Center utilizing a verimax procedure converged in six iterations. The rotated factor matrix, yielding six common factors, is presented in Table 8. Only loadings above .31 (customary) are reported (with the exception of pertinent variables 3 and 16, where the highest loading is used) in order to avoid data of less importance. Loadings above this score account for more than ten percent of the variance.

Grouping by Factor Analysis

The principal results of the factor analysis are presented in the following groups. The individual loadings precede the variables. These may be looked upon as a ranking within each factor.

Factor I: Favorable School Leadership

1. .76—the chief school administrator a leader in the development of a school desegregation plan
2. .69—support by the school board for school desegregation
3. .69—support by the chief school administrator for the school desegregation plan

Factor II: The Opposition

1. .77—opposition to school desegration by the governor
2. .73—opposition to school desegregation by outside organizations
3. .64—opposition to school desegregation by local organizations
4. .60—opposition to school desegregation by the state education department
5. .37—opposition to school desegregation by local individuals

Factor III: The Urban Center

1. .68—larger communities
2. .65—Negroes on the police force

TABLE 8

THE VERIMAX FACTOR MATRIX, NONVIOLENT SCHOOL DESEGREGATION

Row/Col.	I	II	III	IV	V	VI
1. Voluntary School Desegregation				.67		
2. Smaller Communities			.68			
3. High Employment Levels of the Male, Non-White Population				.24		
4. No Police on Duty in Plain Clothes			.55			
5. No Negroes on Police Force			.65			
6. Desegregated Labor Unions						.49
7. Support by Local Newspapers					.36	
8. Support by Respected White Community (Non-political) Members					.49	
9. Nearby Desegregated Public Schools				.31		
10. Comparable Negro and White Schools			.36			
11. The Chief School Administrator a Leader in the Development of a School Desegregation Plan	.76					
12. Support by the Chief School Administrator for the School Desegregation Plan	.70					
13. Support by the School Board for School Desegregation	.70					
14. Preparation by the White Faculty of White Students				.38		
15. Support by State Educational Agencies						.42
16. A Lack of Schools Desegregated at the Same Time			-.28			
17. Desegregation of School Transportation Facilities					.46	
18. Support by White Clergy					.59	
19. Individuals Opposed to School Desegregation		.37				
20. The Governor Opposed to School Desegregation		.77				
21. Local Organizations Opposed to School Desegregation		.64				
22. Outside Organizations Opposed to School Desegregation		.73				
23. Opposition by the State Education Department		.60				

TABLE 9

THE VERIMAX CUMULATIVE SCORE

	Per Cent	Cumulative Per Cent
I	21.03	21.03
II	23.66	44.70
III	18.19	62.88
IV	12.10	74.98
V	15.92	90.90
VI	9.10	100.00

3. .55—police on duty in plain clothes
4. .36—comparable Negro and white schools
5. −.28—a lack of schools desegregated at the same time

Factor IV: The Practical Community

1. .67—voluntary school desegregation
2. .38—preparation by the white faculty of white students for nonviolent school desegregation
3. .31—nearby desegregated public schools
4. .24—high employment of the male, nonwhite population

Factor V: Active Community Support

1. .59—support by the white clergy for school desegregation
2. .49—support by respected white (nonpolitical) community members for nonviolent school desegregation
3. .46—desegregation of school transportation facilities
4. .36—support by local newspapers of nonviolent desegregation

Factor VI: Residual Support

1. .49—desegregated labor unions
2. .42—support by the state educational agencies of school desegregation

Discussion

The arbitrary limit of six factors provided limits for the factor matrix, allowed for sufficient specificity and reduced the amount of less important material reported. One of the questions raised in connection with studies of this type is the grouping of variables. Hopefully, the correlation and factor matrices help clarify these questions.

The factor groupings allowed me to describe pertinent variables in the context of more meaningful factors in the following chapter. These social constructs also provide a clearer context for further questioning and research.

The six factors have been labeled to provide general consistency and meaning under the influence of their various loadings.

Factor I:. Favorable School Leadership—Strong communality is evident in this grouping. The roles of the school administrator and school board clearly dominate.

Factor II: The Opposition—This factor presents a negative conception of school desegregation. Sides are clearly drawn by the variables presented here. Only by their lack of active opposition can they contribute to peaceful school desegregation.

Factor III: The Urban Center—Large size alone seems to make a significant contribution toward violence. Correlating with this variable are *Negroes on the police force* and *the presence of police in plain clothes.*

Factor IV: The Practical Community—The practical community has voluntarily desegregated its schools and has had the white faculty attempt to prepare the white students for nonviolent school desegregation.

Factor V: Active Community Support—Support by three community segments dominate factor V. The white clergy, other respected community leaders, and the local newspapers all share in their efforts here.

Factor VI: Residual Support—Although there was no overwhelming dominance in Factor VI, a background of well-being seems to be making a contribution. The desegregation of labor unions and the practices of the state educational agencies join ranks as a residual force.

A detailed explanation of these factors is given in the following chapter.

III

A Discussion of Factors Associated with Nonviolent Public School Desegregation

Factors associated with peaceful public school desegregation have been identified in the preceding chapter. Some examples are now provided in the hope that they will lead to a more comprehensive understanding of the factors in operation. These examples are provided for clarification, and they may be found helpful to those faced with implementing school desegregation. In each case the examples are based on actual experience. Educators in each school district, though, will need to assess their situation to determine which of the following have application in their situation, and emphasis can be expected to vary from school community to school community.

The identified pertinent factors indicate these things:

1. Multiple variables are closely related.
2. Many people are involved.
3. A community pattern conductive to nonviolent school desegregation can be nurtured by thoughtful and action-orientated educators.
4. Various avenues of positive action are open to different segments of the population that recognize and accept a commitment to social change.

Factor I: Favorable School Leadership

Actions supporting nonviolent school desegregation by the chief school administrator and the social board are closely linked. At times, it would be difficult to determine which of the two initiated action or which was the most effective in influencing policy. To a degree, their roles will be presented separately here. Where they have been merged, no attempt will be made to separate them.

The School Administrator

The chief school administrator had a direct, immediate role as a public agent in school desegregation. His early role in this capacity has been described in Williams and Ryan.[1] Contacts in this study have indicated the importance of the role of the chief school administrator in this question. A statement in the questionnaire returned by G. A. Johnson, a NAACP contact in Delaware, illustrated acceptance and appreciation of the administrator's role.

> Dr. [———], superintendent at that time, worked quietly with the local board of education, which favored a more conservative approach than did Dr. [———]. He also advised against undue publicity. He carefully avoided sensational publicity but kept all school people well informed (about the steps considered for school desegregation).

Another statement from a questionnaire also illustrated appreciation of the administrator's role.

> The school superintendent and administration made significant difference in the community's school desegregation. The principals and teachers of both races have been most helpful.

Other illustrations and examples of action by school administrators follow:

The administrator can apparently exercise some control of newspaper coverage so that the entire procedure is kept manageable. And the wise administrator, as this report shows, was sensitive to both the volume and content of news releases and feature stories.

> On one occasion when requested by a local newspaper to allow them to visit the school and take pictures of the Negro children, we told them that if they planned to take pictures of all the Greek, Italian, several Japanese and a couple of other nationalities represented by our student body, then they could go ahead but they could not single out the Negro children.[2]

The administration can promote the introduction of information into social studies courses about the Negroes' role in American history. The history of the struggle of individual and civil rights might also be included.

The school administrator can meet directly with interracial groups in an attempt to resolve school desegregation controversy. Strong efforts may be

---

[1] Williams, pp. 220-229.

[2] Description provided by a school superintendent.

made for a total drive to improve education under the impetus of school desegregation changes and so create a more favorable climate of opinion.

Establishing an open communications network with the leadership of the Negro community was vital to bringing unity from diversity. When incidents of stress appeared, the previously developed communication pattern between educators and Negroes was an effective means of avoiding unnecessary clashes and conflict. Positive steps have been taken with a beneficial effect on the community to modify policies and change practices to compensate for the disadvantaged situation of Negro youth. By considering valid objections of Negroes concerning school practices and making appropriate adjustments, peaceful desegregation can be accomplished.

In this regard, recommendations by New York City Superintendent of Schools and the Board of Education include—

1. elimination of the group intelligence test and the substitution for it of more valid indicators of ability
2. elimination of short-time instruction or double sessions
3. reduction of class size in selected schools
4. strengthening of the kindergarten and pre-kindergarten programs
5. improvement of the reading and language arts program
6. intensification of programs to reduce dropouts and to assist out-of-school youth to return to school
7. review of the academic and vocational high school instructional program to determine its effectiveness and to provide greater opportunities for minority groups
8. improved programs for recruitment and promotion of Negro and Puerto Rican teachers and supervisors
9. more equitable distribution of experienced teachers and supervisors
10. additional guidance and clinical services where needed
11. scheduled annual standardized achievement tests with results made public
12. expansion of summer school services
13. evaluation of after-school study program
14. strengthening of bilingualism and biculturalism
15. publication of suitable instructional materials depicting good human relations and contributions of minority groups to American history and culture
16. intensification of the present study of textbooks and supplementary materials with a view to eliminating all those which misrepresent minority-group life, history, and contributions
17. improvement of pupil grouping policies
18. greater use of community assistance in voluntary programs
19. increased curricular emphasis on civil liberties
20. extension of team teaching as one approach to meeting the special educational needs of pupils in minority-group areas[3]

---

[3] *Curriculum and Materials* (N.Y.C. Board of Education), Spring, 1964, p. 5.

Fred Hechinger, of the *New York Times*, has pointed out the lack of strong education leadership in the civil rights issue.[4]

1. At best, education reacts to pressures of society, usually after the crisis has become acute, rather than taking the initiative to avert crises.
2. Even with the situation already critical, the leadership-at-large fails to grasp the seriousness and the immediacy of the situation.

Acknowledging this general criticism, many courageous school officials have acted, often in the face of community apathy or criticism. In addition to the activities stated above, the chief school administrator can design a comprehensive school desegregation plan. He can exercise "firm guidance" in all phases of its acceptance. He can influence the school board to accept his plan and then meet with community leaders in an effort to gain their support. Both planning for desegregation and involving a large and diverse group of people in implementing desegregation policies were characteristic of those who demonstrated effective leadership in their communities.

Active support by the clergy, as well as support by community organizations, can also be sought. Strong overtures to the white students can be made for their support of the program. Full support by Negro groups must be continually sought. These elements are some of the aspects of a school desegregation program of White Plains, New York, which achieved commendations from as far away as California.

The chief school administrator can contact interested parties and the general public and appeal to their "higher ideals." A letter forwarded by J. Crockett Farrell, Superintendent of Schools in Florida, is an example of this approach.

> We are rapidly approaching a time when character and leadership will be required and called upon, perhaps as never before. . . .
>
> No school desegregation plan has been proved perfect, but we believe that this step-by-step, gradual effort will be most satisfactory for all persons concerned.
>
> Hillsborough County can be proud of its past record in dealing with interracial matters. Certainly, as long as two men exist, there will be differences of opinion. It cannot be otherwise in a democracy.
>
> But let us, as adults, remember our duty to uphold the law and to work constantly toward progress. Most important, let us remember that the one vital interest should be the children. We have an awesome challenge to guide them throughout their formative years. . . .[5]

---

[4] Fred M. Hechinger, "Failure Up Front," *The New York Times* (Feb. 23, 1964), p. E 7.

[5] J. Crockett Farrell, Superintendent of Public Instruction, Tampa, Florida, "Letter to Interested Parties", August 20, 1963.

To summarize, with the words of Dr. Robin Williams, Jr.—

> School officials must have clear, forthright policies with firm leadership. . . . There are no problems of a racial, national or religious nature in a community that cannot be managed by the people of a community and school officials. . . . Of first importance is attention to the welfare of all the children of the community. . . . Community actions and examples are important in order to teach tolerance. . . . Frequently, the school can and has successfully taken the leadership in achieving school desegregation. . . . We must provide opportunities for direct experiences to break down stereotypes.[6]

The School Board

The role of the school board, as stated earlier, is woven with that of the chief school administrator and is of the greatest importance. The respondent in one community said this:

> Our school board took this position before all community groups and organizations: It isn't a question of whether you like it or don't like it. The question is: shall we desegregate peacefully and with dignity or shall we go out of the public school business? Except for isolated individuals, here and there, our community decided overwhelmingly that we would operate public schools.

In several communities the decision was influenced by the economics involved. The school board decided that it simply became too costly to operate a dual school system. A community contact phrased it this way:

> School desegregation in our community was handled as if it were a matter of fact routine matter. The decisions by the local Board of Education was announced as a result of a study by the group to help solve financial problems.

A common rationale found among other logical ideas in support of desegregation is reflected in this quote: "It simply became too expensive to run a dual educational system."

Another community contact indicated that the only "group or event" that made a significant difference in their school desegregation was their school board. In describing this action he stated—

> We made no issue whatever about our desegregation. We invited a committee of five colored leaders before the board and planned a procedure as follows: that the colored people obtain the services of an NAACP attorney and file for desegregation—we would cooperate with them. . . .
>
> We believe that too many times issues are made on this thing which creates conflicts. We believe the best way is to just desegregate the shortest way with the least time. Creating committees, advisory groups, etc., just invites trouble.

---

[6] Dr. Robin Williams, Jr., Address to the P.T.A. Institute at Cornell University, April 24, 1963.

One of the contacts forwarded a lengthy dispatch describing in full the role of the community school board in achieving nonviolent school desegregation. It seems worthy of summary at this point.

A definite plan should be established and followed without regard to lay opposition. The board, as the legal representative of the schools, should be the power making all decisions affecting schools. These decisions should be carefully thought out. Once made, they should be adhered to firmly.

"Common sense in face of the inevitable" should be a guide, but loyalty to social patterns must be considered. All publicity concerning the desegregation should be factual; all individuals concerned should be treated with respect and dignity.

The final decision must be followed without exception in the individual schools. Once the change was made, students of both races were to be treated alike, with the same rights and duties.

Also, there should be a good legal counselor available whose advice should be followed. Legal counsel was often wisely sought as the strategy for desegregation was developed, and not added after an explosive situation arose.

A further example of the interrelationship between the school board and the school administration is contained in the report of a community where their roles, in this regard, are considered as one.

> School board and administration, by personal, word of mouth interaction, convinced business and civil leaders that the action was necessary, feasible, and inevitable. The board then revised policy to provide for placement of pupils without regard to race.
>
> Joint and separate meetings of colored and white parents were scheduled, and school programs were explained, as well as a thorough discussion of plans for the desegregation. All questions were answered.

Factor I presents a pattern of strong school leadership. This leadership was a decisive force in nonviolent school desegregation. Within such a construct, school personnel cannot abdicate the responsibility of leadership. Firmness, thoughtfulness, and consideration appear to be the guiding principles. Respect for all parties must never be forgotten, regardless of traditional differences of views.

Factor II: The Opposition

Opposition, which was identified with the violent communities, came from the governor, local and outside organizations, local individuals, and the state education department. Neither compromise nor understanding was apparent in the communities. The uncompromising governor was a prime force.

The Governor

In September 1963 Governor Wallace of Alabama stated:

> There now exists in the state of Alabama conditions (court ordered school desegregation) calculated to result in a disruption of the peace and tranquility of this State, and to occasion peril to the lives and property of the citizens. . . .[7]

Within two days Birmingham was rocked by violence. Interestingly enough, the Governor's actions of opposition to school desegregation were opposed by "local school boards and officials, and by parents and others in the affected cities."[8] Yet, in April of 1967 Governor Lurleen Wallace still resisted the inevitability of genuine school desegregation.

In Mississippi, Governor Barnett's inflammatory remarks were generally conceded to have played a significant part in the violence at the University of Mississippi at the time of the admission of James Meredith.[9] While political leaders have inflamed peaceful integration practices, educators have sometimes quietly, yet firmly, led their communities into acceptance programs of desegregation.

For the most part, specific statements by these governors requested nonviolence. However, their "racist" views, their attacks on the federal government, their linking Communism with desegregation, and their insistence on preserving the "Southern way" all seemed to contribute to an atmosphere fraught with violence. It is difficult to perceive how Governor Wallace's policy of "segregation today, segregation tomorrow, segregation forever" left any room for accommodation or compromise.

This summary does not imply that the approach adopted by all Southern and border states' governors provoked violence. At the Southern Governors' Parley at White Sulphur Springs, West Virginia, in August 1963, only two of these governors, Wallace and Barnett, sought a showdown on the desegregation issue. A moderate tendency expressed by the other governors was far more evident.

An example of a positive approach to the issue was provided by Governor Hollings of South Carolina.

---

[7] "Wallace Halts Negroes at Schools," *Southern School News*, quoting Gov. George Wallace, September, 1963, p. 2.

[8] "Governor Bars Negroes Entry at Three Schools," *ibid.*, p. 1.

[9] *New York Times School Weekly*, October 7, 1962, p. 7.

The Governor presented three guidelines to his legal counsel for the desegregation of Clemson College:

1. The plan must be foolproof; there should be no question of the need for U.S. marshals;
2. It should be designed to prevent even the possibility of allowing a crowd to gather, and
3. A carefully thoughtout schedule must be arranged for controlling the movement of the press.[10]

In a farewell address to the state legislature, the Governor stated—

> South Carolina is running out of courts. This General Assembly must make clear South Carolina's choice, a government of laws rather than a government of men. We must move on with dignity. It must be done with law and order. The state's institutions and all law enforcement agencies have been charged with their responsibilities.[11]

The desegregation of Clemson College could be used as a model for dignified and nonviolent desegregation.

In a contrary, uncompromising position, Governor Faubus had stated that if Negroes tried to desegregate the schools of Little Rock, Arkansas, the "blood will run in the streets." It did. In the last two cases, the final result was desegregation; the difference in attitude by the governors could scarcely have provided a sharper dichotomy.

Organizations

Opposition by local and outside organizations were also identified by the study of matched communities as associated with violence. At least fifty different types of pro-segregationist organizations have operated in the South since 1954. The results of this study point out their relationship to school violence in recent years.

It seems important to review some of the ways these organizations have functioned in the past in their active opposition to school desegregaion proceedings:

They have issued bulletins condemning school desegregation and indicated that this desegregation was but a step on the way to the loss of the white man's job.

---

[10] George McMillan, "Integration With Dignity," *Saturday Evening Post*, March 16, 1963, p. 18.

[11] *Ibid.*, p. 18.

They have burned crosses in an effort to intimidate communities facing school desegregation.

They have attempted to organize massive resistance to school desegregation efforts, specifically stating that violence was to be used as one of their weapons.

They have supported and voted for segregationist candidates at all civic levels.

They have boycotted businesses employing Negroes.

They have castrated a Negro as a "lesson" to a Negro community seeking school desegregation.

They have participated in church bombings, whippings, and beatings as part of their anti-desegregation battle.

They have sought to provoke anger and resort-to-violence movements without hesitation.

They have attempted to organize many right-wing groups to combat desegregation "legally so far as we can and violently when necessary."

The State Education Department

The study of matched communities also indicated that opposition by the state education department was correlated with violence in school desegregation. But rather than indicate the actions and attitudes by the departments of education which hindered school desegregation, let's consider some of the steps which are favorable to nonviolence—steps which some departments have already taken in a number of instances.

A state department of education, through its commissioner, can appoint an Advisory Committee on Human Rights to help ease the transitional period. This committee may advise and help individual communities desegregating their schools.

The department can issue statements indicating the advantages of school desegregation to all races concerned. The weight of the state's influence can be of real help to local school boards as their plans for desegregation are developed and implemented.

The department can stress the social equality of all children and the need for an active acceptance of respect for all children.

The departments can ask local boards for—

> A statement of policy by your board of education with respect to the maintenance of racial balance in your schools.
>
> In districts where racial imbalance exists, or is a problem, a report of progress made toward eliminating it.

In such districts, your plan for further action, including estimates of additional cost, if any, and of the time required for carrying out your plan.[12]

In other words, where possible, the full weight of the state department of education can support the nonviolent school desegregation drive.

The duty of the state department of education need not stop with support and recommendations. In addition, for example, the department can provide lists of books, pamphlets, articles, and films which would help develop a spirit of understanding and which might be used by school systems before and after school desegregation to further racial understanding.[13]

Among the recommended books might be *The Fears Men Live By* by Selma Hirsh (Harper and Brothers, 1955); *The Negro Potential* by Eli Ginzberg (Columbia University Press, 1956); *The Negro Vanguard* by Richard Bardolph (Rinehart and Co., 1959); and *To Kill a Mockingbird* by Harper Lee (J. B. Lippincott Co., 1960).

It is unfortunate that the policies of the state departments of education and the school administrators (Factor I) were often in opposition to each other. Physical proximity to the state capital and additional political sensitivity in this position may have hindered a more positive role by the state education departments. A more favorable climate of opinion should enable the state leadership to match the positive action of some administrators and some boards of education at the local level in achieving a transition that is nonviolent.

Individuals

The study of matched communities also indicated the important role of local individuals opposed to school desegregation who were not functioning as members of pro-segregationist organizations. Their activities also correlated with violence—violence which was expressed in many ways:

At times, it was led and expressed by teenagers who reacted strongly and fearfully against change.

At times, it was provoked by a community leader with a history of segregationist sentiment who would not compromise.

At times, it has been manifested in mobs reacting violently on the opening day of a desegregated school.

---

[12] The Commissioner of Education, "Racial Imbalance in Schools," Albany, New York: The State Education Department, June 14, 1963, p. 2.

[13] Nida E. Thomas, "Intercultural Relations: A Suggested Reading List," *The Bookmark*, Albany, New York: The State Education Department, March 1962, p. 163.

At times, it has manifested itself through violent white response to Negro demonstrations seeking faster desegregation.

At times, it has manifested itself in bombings, retaliation against school desegregation. Violence of this magnitude caused a white lawyer in Birmingham to declare—

> Who did it? . . . It is the coward in each of us who clucks admonitions. We are ten years of lawless preachments, ten years of criticism of law, of courts, of our fellow man; a decade of telling school children the opposite of what the civics say. We are a mass of intolerance and bigotry and stand indicted before our youth.[14]

At times, it has manifested itself in the murder of a Negro desegregationist leader.

This is not to suggest that the opposition has always been permitted to manifest itself in violence. An account of the desegregation of Atlanta schools shows how much control is possible:

> And, finally, it is the story of a plan for the opening days of school, conceived by the administrative staff of the schools and executed, under the scrutiny of the police department, with a meticulosity of detail characterizing the D-Day landings. The crank, the crackpot, the lunatic fringe—homegrown and imported—didn't have an opportunity, not a prayer of a chance, to be himself. For a few days, at least, he was a model citizen.[15]

Fortunately, only a small percentage of the citizens of the Southern and border states are advocates of violent opposition to school desegregation. Where variables associated with violence have been isolated, they have been listed and discussed in this study so that those interested may learn what to expect and can plan action that would remedy a difficult situation. Perhaps former Governor of Florida, Leroy Collins, has placed this factor in proper perspective:

> Leroy Collins . . . urged Southerners tonight to tell "the bloody-shirt wavers to climb off the buckboards of bigotry" . . . "for too long have we permitted the South's own worst enemies to speak for it. . . .
>
> How long are the majority of Southerners going to allow themselves to be caricatured before the nation by these Claghorns? . . .

---

[14] Charles Morgan, Jr., "Talk Before Young Men's Business Club," reported in *Life*, September 27, 1963, p. 44B.

[15] *The Atlanta Desegregation Story: A Synopsis*, The Atlanta Public Schools, undated, p. 1.

I say to you tonight that above all else it is the moral duty of our generation to plow under racial injustice everywhere in the United States. . . ."[16]

Factor III: The Urban Center

The urban center provides a setting conducive to violent school desegregation. With a multitude of people of various backgrounds it is difficult to perceive how the suggested prerequisites for nonviolent change—communication in good faith and an understanding attitude—can be easily achieved. The value and importance of the urban center make the outcome of the desegregation issue of great importance to both sides, both the segregationist and the desegregationist. Because of its significance, the great numbers of people involved, the urban center has become a crucial battleground for these opposing ideologies.

The Significance of Size

The large size of the community has been associated with the tendency toward violence during school desegregation. In this study five of the seven violent communities had populations of at least 50,000 persons. This is not to say, of course, that every large community will automatically be subjected to violent school desegregation. It is to say, however, that larger communities have more often experienced violence in this area, and if violence is to be avoided in school desegregation in larger communities, greater vigilance should be exercised.

There are, most likely, several influences in the relationship between violence and urban desegregation. For one, there may be a rising percentage of Negroes in urban areas. This rising population can cause anxiety in the white masses who fear that they will soon be in the minority. It is evident that many of our urban centers will have Negro majorities by 1970. With this abundance of Negroes it is no longer a case of permitting a small percent of a "minority" group to go to school with the majority. Rather, it may mean that the white group will become the minority group. Hence, local whites may believe that there is good reason to resist school desegregation. Such a situation may exist in a community of any size, but the recent migration of Negroes has been toward the cities.

Many people seem to fear that school desegregation could also be a forerunner to political oblivion for urban, minority whites, a second influence in

[16] *New York Times*, "Collins Urges South to Muffle Bigots Who Act as Spokesmen," December 4, 1963, p. 19.

the drive to maintain segregation (and subjugation) for as long as possible.

A third influence may lie in the fact that, in larger communities, Negro organizations exist which have the means to press for civil rights. It is expected that this action would be opposed by segregationists, both individuals and organizations. This action might help to explain increased violence in urban areas. Perhaps a lack of desegregationist action by Negro organizations would help maintain tranquility, but however desirable peace is, it cannot always be recommended if it means the denial of legal and civil rights. The achievement of both, nonviolence and civil rights, is the greater goal.

Basic to the phenomenon of violence is the structure and size of the community itself. In Williams' listing of propositions concerning racial relations we find the following:

> 21. The greater the differentiation of groups and of individual social roles in a society, the greater the probabilities of group conflict.
> 22. Intergroup conflict is the most likely the more rapid and far reaching the social changes to which individuals have to adjust.[17]

In both propositions we find tendencies for largeness to correlate with conflict, especially at a time when drastic social changes are in progress. People newly arrived in urban areas must make adjustments to housing differences, recreational changes, transportation differences, and work opportunities. Even the family roles may be different.

The statistical evidence of the study of matched communities has associated largeness with violence. Awareness of this relationship provides a warning and a stimulus for remedial action; the existence of this relationship is not an excuse for the prediction and acceptance of inevitable chaos.

Negroes on the Police Force

In six of the seven violent communities isolated in this study, Negroes were employed on the police force. Yet, Wey and Corey have described the effectiveness of a biracial police department.[18] It must be noted that Rev. Dr. Martin Luther King, Jr., used his influence to continue Negro demonstrations in Birmingham, Alabama, as a lever in demanding that Negroes be admitted to the police force. Dr. King achieved this goal. Although this goal is one of importance in achieving racial dignity, in providing jobs, and in possibly

---

[17] Robin M. Williams, Jr., *The Reduction of Intergroup Tension* (New York: Social Science Research Council, 1947), p. 56.

[18] Herbert Wey and John Corey, *Action Patterns in School Desegregation* (Bloomington, Indiana: Phi Delta Kappa, Inc., 1959), p. 191.

reducing police brutality to Negroes, there is no evidence that this situation aids in producing nonviolent school desegregation.

It is possible that when tempers are high, the presence of Negroes in police uniform provides an additional disturbing factor to segregationists. In answer to a query on this point, however, one source said, "the utilization of the individuals enumerated in your letter [Negroes on the police force and police in plain clothes] contributed in no way to racial unrest.'[19] (For additional confirmation see Appendix E.)

It might be speculated, with support from the above quote and other statements obtained in this study, that the relationship between Negroes on the police force and school violence is purely coincidental. Possibly Negroes press for admittance to the police force because of intolerable social conditions, the same conditions which may contribute to community violence during school desegregation. One might also argue that Negroes on the police force are an index of a progressive community. The association with violence exists because a community in change may be more likely to experience conflict. Considering all the evidence, it appears that, if properly handled, Negroes on the police force do not contribute to violence.

Police in Plain Clothes

There is a significant correlation between police on duty in plain clothes and property damage. Yet most students of the subject would likely agree with Wey and Corey that the "use of plain clothes men [is] advised."[20] In this study, five of the seven violent communities utilized police in plain clothes at the time of school desegregation. Perhaps these police were on duty in plain clothes because violence was expected, and their action may not have been sufficient to prevent the inception of violence. The statement from a community contact, previously noted, as well as other contacts, would suggest that these plainclothesmen contributed in no way to racial unrest.

It might be argued that effective action by uniformed police would more easily convince a crowd that restraints were being imposed and that the police fully intended to keep the situation under control. One possible interpretation is that in locating leaders of potential violence the use of plainclothesmen is advisable, but that, in seeking to directly control mobs or violence, utilization of uniformed police should be of primary importance. Again, after analysis of all the data, it is reasonable to conclude that the rela-

---

[19] Wm. Henry Oliver, Co-Superintendent of Schools, Nashville, Tennessee.
[20] Wey and Corey, *Action Patterns*, p. 195.

tionship of police on duty in plain clothes is purely a chance relationship and is possibly most indicative of a community which is mustering all possible strength to stop expected trouble.

Comparison of Negro and White Facilities

There is a correlation between communities with comparable Negro and white schools and nonviolent desegregation of these schools. In these instances buildings and equipment of both systems were judged to be approximately equal. The author can locate no examples, despite the correlation.

The author located information revealing that equal expenditures for Negro and white statewide school systems have not existed in any of the Southern states. Since the Supreme Court decision of 1954, the trend has been to close the gap, often with the hope of stalling desegregation. Unfortunately for those who desire an equality of expenditures, "there is an apparent trend in allocations for a decrease in the rate of closing the gap as the expenditures for Negroes approach those for whites.[21]

The Influence of Concurrent Desegregation

The last variable included in this factor indicates that there was a lack of nearby schools desegregating at the time of violent school desegregation in the community being investigated. Where there has been massive resistance, desegregation has been extremely slow.

The extremely slow desegregation rates of Alabama and Mississippi certainly point out this tendency. This resistance can easily account for both the violence and the lack of nearby schools desegregating at the same time. It appears to be conducive to nonviolence if several nearby school districts or schools planning to desegregate take the step together.

> When only one school in an area desegregates at a time, outside racists can mobilize and incite irresponsible forces against the school concerned. When several school districts in the same area are desegregated at the same time, the rabble rousers must divide forces and thus lose power. A common question asked by parents in school districts that have desegregated when other districts around them have not was, "Why do we have to desegregate our schools when neighbors are not doing it?"
>
> On the positive side, it is apparent that the strongest bulwark of defense is multi-school unity.[22]

---

[21] Carroll L. Miller, "Educational Opportunities and the Negro Child in the South," *Harvard Educational Review*, Summer, 1960, p. 197.

[22] Wey and Corey, *Action Patterns*, p. 138.

Factor IV: The Practical Community

The practical community, as defined here, is one which has taken substantial positive action in an effort to insure an orderly school desegregation. The practical community is dominated by the fact that its schools desegregated as a result of voluntary rather than special court ordered desegregation specifically aimed at their community. These communities are not necessarily seeking or advocating school desegregation but have assessed the social climate and have completed the inevitable transition with nonviolence and dignity. A respondent in a community discussed why his community desegregated its schools voluntarily:

> The [———] schools were desegregated "voluntarily" to prevent the Negroes from carrying the case to court. There was fear by the school board that the city would lose the case in court and that the court would prescribe a plan for the board to operate under.

The above statement is supported by an Associated Press dispatch from Greenville, South Carolina, indicating that their voluntary school desegregation was carried out "with the knowledge that the trial of a pending desegregation suit might have resulted in a stronger integration order."[23] Under their new policy, race and color were no longer to be considered factors in student assignment and transfer.

Other schools have apparently desegregated, not in fear of a court decision, but simply as a matter of course. They believed that the time had come for such action, and they were willing to take the initiative. It is because of this willingness to go along with the inevitable, to make easier what they probably could not avoid, to follow "a natural process," that Factor IV is labeled *the practical community.*

The Preparation of White Students

The practical community also asked their white teachers to prepare their white students for desegregation. It was probably predicted that class discussion of the situation might help pave the way for nonviolent desegregation. The teacher might provide learning situations, supply information and material,[24] and introduce—

---

[23] AP, "School Integration Approved by Court in Greenville, S. C.," *New York Times* (April 28, 1964), p. 27.

[24] Material listed under the role of the State Education Department, Factor II, can provide a beginning.

. . . general discussions on such subjects as the propaganda techniques used by hate groups, when and how children learn to hate people different from themselves, the value of human differences in our society, the implications of the Bill of Rights for everyone, the meaning of cultural pluralism, the responsibility of the individual for the maintenance and improvement of democracy.[25]

The teacher might also—

1. read and analyze documents and laws relating to civil rights
2. work with the student council in a project designed to develop a Human Relations Program for the school
3. indicate the economic loss to the locality, the state, and the nation because of discrimination
4. indicate the restrictive effects of discrimination and the impoverishment it brings to all concerned
5. point out that in a democracy the integrity and dignity of each person is crucial[26]
6. utilize films which might help clarify the problem and support previous positive attitudes

Some recommended films are *Americans All, Boundary Lines, Brotherhood of Man,* and *Cast the First Stone.*[27]

The Importance of Previous Desegregation

There is also a positive correlation between nonviolent school desegregation and nearby previously desegregated schools. This author believes that many of the illustrations pertaining to voluntary school desegregation also apply to the positive relationship of nearby desegregated public schools. Having nearby desegregated schools gave the community the secure feeling that they were not pioneering in this area and that the desegregation of their schools was "developing as a natural process in this community."

A respondent from a community with nearby desegregated public schools phrased it in this way: "There was a general feeling in the community that the time had come to integrate. There was no open opposition."

A bandwagon effect, or just a willingness to bow to the inevitable, seems to be considerably enhanced by the presence of nearby desegregated public schools. The correlation between this situation and nonviolence is statistically confirmed.

---

[25] Gertrude Noar, *Prejudices and Discrimination* (New York: The Anti-Defamation League of B'nai B'rith, undated), pp. 22, 23.

[26] *Ibid.*, summary of key points.

[27] Ashley Montagu, *What We Know About "Race"* (New York: The Anti-Defamation League of B'nai B'rith, undated) "Teacher's Supplement," p. 6.

Employment

A fourth characteristic of the practical community is above average employment (for that community) of the male nonwhite population. Nationally, we have been experiencing a period when nonwhite unemployment runs two or more times that of white unemployment. Under such broad circumstances it is of interest to note that in a community where high employment of nonwhites exists, we find a correlation with nonviolent school desegregation. This above average nonwhite employment possibly indicates equally high white employment and, hence, communities enjoying economic health, although they are not sufficiently different from violent communities to produce a statistical difference in these other areas. It is possible that under these favorable economic conditions, the fear of competition for jobs is not critical and positive steps toward school desegregation can be more easily put into effect.

What, then, are some of the steps which have been taken to aid nonwhite employment (fully recognizing that employment of the total labor force is probably the more important consideration)?

1. The Federal Government has stepped up the hiring of nonwhites under its Fair Hiring Policy.
2. The President's Committee on Equal Employment Opportunity has applied pressure where job bias is found in major industries and apprentice programs.
3. Federal action has encouraged the teaching of job skills, provided employment offices, and expanded work study programs.
4. The Federal Government has, itself, provided jobs and money for retraining, as a stimulus to job growth when the need is great.
5. Some states have opened up "lines of communication between Negroes and whites," encouraged Negro proposals, and stimulated business concern and responsibility. Individual states have also launched programs of their own, including preschool programs, counseling and job training, and adult education courses. North Carolina is a worthy example of this.
6. City administrators have helped by providing additional social workers to combat basic family, social, and economic problems, removing bias in hiring, and hiring more minority group members than previously.
7. Civic-minded organizations have assisted in job training and placement.
8. Schools have provided more and better guidance and opened the schools for job training and cultural activities.
9. Dropout rehabilitation programs have been instituted to reclaim lost potential.

10. Community educational systems have started early recruitment drives in an effort to increase the number of Negro teachers in their systems.
11. Clergymen have attacked job bias.
12. Intergroup organizations have pressed antibias job campaigns through consultation, boycotts, and sermons.
13. Businessmen have provided additional job training and have increased their rate of hiring Negroes in better skilled jobs.

These suggestions should not be considered final resolutions but rather a beginning, if Negro attainment of fair employment and a good education is to become a reality.

The need for greater fulfillment of these recommendations is evident when one realizes that even with these successful beginnings the mean income between Negro and white families is still widening. Educators, in many communities, have worked consistently and forcefully to provide compensatory educational opportunities for Negro youth to reduce the race gap in educational and socioeconomic areas.

Factor V: Active Community Support

The community which actively supports school desegregation finds its moderates speaking out in support of nonviolent school desegregation. Apparently, not all of this support is rendered because of a belief in the morality of the act. While the white clergy may render support because of moral principles, the white community members and newspapers generally support nonviolent desegregation as the wisest move in the face of the inevitable. From either point of view, effective support is provided. However, before this support was often given, educators had to seek it.

The Church Leaders

This reply to one of the items on a questionnaire provides an example of the role white church leaders can play: "A special group of leading ministers (white) met with a special group of Negroes. These leaders, I think, helped to absorb and soften what could have been a jolting and shocking impact."

It would be naive, however, to believe that in the ministry, or in any profession which requires interaction with the public, there is always a course toward the good and the true.

> I've preached some (sermons for integration) in this vein, but the thing is that I've never moved anyone's opinion with it. The response I've gotten is that

I was berating the congregation from the privileged sanctuary of the pulpit when they couldn't answer back.

And so I have come to terms with the limitations of the minister's role. I read articles critical of the minister for not giving leadership to his community. Does anyone really believe that the community in general and the power structure in particular will reverently bow their heads in obedience if a pastor tells them what their attitudes on a given course of action should be? Our society just doesn't accord that kind of power to ministers; it hasn't since the time of the Puritans.[28]

However, clergymen have found it possible to take the following steps:

1. More than 4,000 clerical representatives of Protestantism, Roman Catholicism, and Judaism attended an interfaith rally in Washington, D.C., supporting the Civil Rights Bill and thus demonstrating to all their position on civil rights and desegregation.
2. Members of the clergy have led a renewed drive for interracial congregations by having church members transfer in both directions.
3. Members of the clergy, as individuals respected by most people, have undertaken more active roles as mediators of racial disputes. These tactics have been commendably utilized in New York City and Savannah, Georgia, and may well be broadened in application.
4. Sunday school lessons and sermons have been written to emphasize the brotherhood of man.
5. Clergymen have taken an active interest in desegregation movements, beginning with church-controlled enterprises, schools, and hospitals.
6. Churchmen have called attention to the moral issues at stake in desegregation proceedings. The following statement from the ministers of Rocky Mount, North Carolina, is an illustration of one way in which this procedure was demonstrated.

We, the undersigned ministers of the Christian gospel, called to serve as pastors and religious leaders of the Rocky Mount community, bear a Special responsibility for the moral and spiritual guidance of its people. We call upon them, and especially upon the members of the churches, to recognize that the dignity of every man is a central teaching of our Lord and Savior Jesus Christ. Wherever human personality is injured by prejudice, discrimination or contempt, the spirit and teaching of Jesus is denied. We call to mind the fact that the Scriptures in both the Old and New Testaments plainly declare God's requirement of justice in all human relations. And we declare our conviction that the life of this

[28] Robert Collie, "A 'Silent Minister' Speaks Up," *New York Times Magazine*, May 24, 1964, p. 12.

nation "under God" requires that we approach all community problems with this sense of moral responsibility.

We recognize that the Church through its ministers and members has long witnessed to the dignity of all men, and that many have labored to promote this gospel in community relations, in business dealings, in the churches and elsewhere. We are grateful for the fact that responsible leaders of both racial groups in our community are now seeking to remove discriminations that still exist, and to achieve these changes with all possible dispatch through means of negotiation and cooperation.

We now therefore call upon all the people of our community to undergird these efforts and urge that they:—

Actively support the leadership of the Mayor's Good Neighbor Committee;

Refuse to be agitated by rumors, but seek to learn the true facts of the situation as it develops;

Seek to promote understanding and the good of the whole community by our conversation and conduct at home and with all our fellow citizens;

Try the more earnestly to bring forth in our own lives the Christian fruits of love, patience, perseverance, and self-discipline;

Pray that the will of God whom we know in Jesus Christ may prevail in our own lives and the life of our community.

7. Churchmen have helped provide men and money to bring to poverty-stricken areas "direct relief, job training, leadership education programs and techniques designed to open up communication between Negroes and whites."[29]
8. Clergymen have written messages with moving eloquence. "The Letter from Birmingham Jail" by Martin Luther King, Jr., is a prime example of this action. Several lines from it are quoted below:

Moreover, I am cognizant of the interrelatedness of communities and states. I cannot sit idly by in Atlanta and not be concerned about what happens in Birmingham. Injustice anywhere is a threat to justice everywhere. We are caught in an inescapable network of mutuality, tied in a single garment of destiny. Whatever affects one directly, affects all indirectly. Never again can we afford to live with the narrow, provincial "outside agitator" idea. Anyone who lives inside the United States can never be considered an outsider anywhere within its bounds.[30]

But the clergy plays its greatest role as mediator. Clergy mediation in racial conflict has functioned successfully. A prime example of successful action by the clergy in Savannah, Georgia.

---

[29] George Dugan, "Churches Attack Poverty in South," *New York Times* (February, 27, 1964), p. 23.

[30] Martin Luther King, Jr., *Why We Can't Wait* (New York: Signet Books, 1963), p. 77.

The city was beset with racial violence, vandalism and rioting. There were shootings and great property damage. Racial conditions were critical. A Monsignor Toomey entered the scene with the hope of bringing about peace through discussion. He extracted a commitment from religious leaders and a promise of cooperation from businessmen. Sales had slumped, and, together, the groups agreed that justice and economics indicated the need for a restoration of order. Toomey's drive restored hope and brought about negotiations from which blossomed peace out of chaos.[31]

This is an example of the positive role of mediation which the clergy can perform. Even in a power structure where the ministry feels compelled to avoid controversy or a desegregationist label, it can still function in its traditional role of peacemaker and mediator. Much additional action of this type seems to be indicated.

White Leadership

In the book *The Negro Revolt*, Louis Lomax describes the refusal of white leadership in Southern communities to speak out favorably on the school desegregation issue:

> We—particularly those of us who were Southern born—had faith in a class of white people known to Negroes as *good white* people. These were the respectable white people who were pillars of the Southern community and who appeared to be the power structure of the community. It never occurred to us that professional white people would let poor white trash storm the town and take over. Not that the good white people wanted integration—indeed, we knew they did not—but we expected them to be law-abiding and to insist that their communities remained that way.[32]

In describing the Negroes' reaction to the silent white leadership Lomax says, "But in the process they have done something even worse; they have destroyed the Negro's faith in the basic integrity of the white power structure."

However, not all were silent. Here are some examples of notable actions by white leaders:

1. A steel company official labored to form a civic group which would aid interracial relations, although he was ousted from his company job for so doing.
2. The mother of a governor was jailed after challenging segregation and in

[31] M. S. Handler, "Savannah Truce Shaped by Priest," *New York Times* (August 4, 1963), p. 64.

[32] Louis E. Lomax, *The Negro Revolt* (New York: Signet Books, 1962), p. 85.

so doing "brought about the unaccustomed weapon of impeccable respectability to bear against the sun-baked seacoast town's oldest convictions."[33]

3. Respected artists have refused to perform before segregated audiences and have thus dramatized their hostility towards segregation.
4. Professor James Silver, a faculty member of the University of Mississippi, serving as an example of academic and professional responsibility, has "befriended James Meredith, ate with him on campus, golfed with him, and invited him home."[34] (James Meredith was the first known Negro to attend the University of Mississippi.)

In criticizing the society about him, Professor Silver said this:

> The totalitarian society of Mississippi imposes on all its people acceptance of an obedience to an official orthodoxy almost identical with the pro-slavery philosophy. . . . Mississippi is the way it is not because of its views on the Negro—here it is simply the South exaggerated—but because of its closed society, its refusal to allow freedom of inquiry or to tolerate error of opinion. . . .
>
> And yet, in spite of all that has been presented in this paper, it seems inescapable that Mississippians one day will drop the mockery of the late confederacy and resume their obligations as Americans. There is small reason to believe that they will somehow develop the capacity to do it themselves, to do it as Faulkner says, in time. If not, the closed society will become the open society with the massive aid of the country as a whole, backed by the power and authority of the federal government.[35]

5. Local attorneys, as professional leaders dedicated to law and justice, have taken an active role in support of minority positions. "Lawyers, whether in private practice or public life, have a grave moral responsibility to participate in the nation's current efforts to deal justly with all its citizens regardless of race, color or creed."[36] In Birmingham, Alabama, fifty-three local lawyers recognized this responsibility and requested that citizens obey the law.[37]

6. Local business leaders have supported the cause of desegregation by voluntarily desegregating "hotels, restaurants, stores and theaters" where possible. In Savannah, Georgia, during the racial crisis, it was claimed

[33] "Mother Goes to Jail," *Newsweek* (April 13, 1964), p. 25.

[34] "Closed Society," *Newsweek* (November 18, 1963), p. 66.

[35] James Silver, "Mississippi: The Closed Society," Presidential Address before the Southern Historical Association, Asheville, N. C., November 7, 1963.

[36] "Lawyers Hear Civil Rights Plea at the Red Mass in St. Patrick's," *New York Times* (October 14, 1963), p. 22.

[37] John Herberg, "53 Lawyers Urge Birmingham Amity," *New York Times* (September 29, 1963), p. 1.

that the business leaders, who in reality held the power to resolve the uneasiness, determined to settle outstanding disputes. In Birmingham, Alabama, it was the business community which applied pressures for racial compromise in order to avert the severe economic damage caused by the racial crisis.

7. Local leaders have supported efforts toward racial peace, even in areas where many do not support desegregation. Again, in Birmingham, this proved possible.

> Faltering though it was, the statement was of some help—if only because it attached the names of Birmingham's "Big Mule" civic and business elite, however half-heartedly, to the truce. As one gaunt elevator operator put it: "You can't do nothing to those men on that list. How can you boycott the Alabama Power Company?"[38]

8. The story of the nonviolent desegregation of Clemson College in South Carolina is an example of successful efforts by respected community leaders to achieve this end. They acted with dignity and an entire community benefitted. Charles Daniel, a local businessman, gathered public support by stating:

> We have a definite obligation to increase the productivity of our Negro citizens, to provide them with good jobs at good wages and to continue to assure them of fair treatment. . . . By raising their education and economic status, we would raise the whole economy of the state.[39]

South Carolina's Governor Hollings was prepared for school desegregation and wished to preserve law and order. He informed newsmen of this in order to prepare the public for the nonviolent course he intended to pursue.

Clemson College Board Chairman Brown committed the board of trustees and the administration to absolute nonviolence on the Clemson campus. Clemson's President Edwards strongly sought to gain the support of possible influential opposition. He asked for their complete support of his actions or he threatened to resign.

South Carolina's State Senator Marion Gressette stated in Senatorial debate his complete commitment to peace and good order. His call for nonviolence was a key to its achievement.

Thus, the combined community forces had succeeded in creating a social setting conducive to the maintenance of peace and order. Compliance with desegregation was not what some of these leaders may have wished for, but

---

[38] "Birmingham's Choice," *Newsweek* (May 26, 1963), p. 26.

[39] George McMillan, "Integration With Dignity," *Saturday Evening Post*, pp. 16, 17.

nonviolence and the preservation of a cohesive community was the higher attained goal.

School Transportation

Another significant variable located in this factor was the desegregation of school transportation systems. No examples of the desegregation of school transportation will be offered since none of the contacts provided insights into this variable, and no meaningful illustrations could be located.

The Role of the Newspaper

Favorable coverage by local newspapers has been indicated as pertinent in achieving nonviolent school desegregation. Some comment has been provided in field responses: "With the cooperation of local news media our desegregation was done quietly."

A community contact gives credit for its nonviolence to "a favorable press and other news media."

Clippings forwarded by a contact in Rocky Mount, North Carolina, illustrate the active role the local newspaper can play by providing favorable coverage.

> There are few things in this world that cannot be settled by peaceful negotiation and certainly our interracial problem is not one of them. Rocky Mount citizens—both white and Negro—can settle any issue, without "help" from the outside, that has arisen or will arise to muddle race relations, and as long as we have such dedicated men as those who comprise the Good Neighbor Committee and men of understanding and a willingness to cooperate as those who expressed themselves at the League meeting, Rocky Mount may well be the city that will set the example for wholesome racial relations in the future.[40]
>
> Let's get behind the mayor in his effort to get citizens to "join together in an effort to relieve the tensions" and let's also adhere to his plea to citizens to "respect the rights of each other." At the same time, let's be extremely wary of rumors, waiting until responsible parties have provided the information sought. Above all, let's keep our sanity; let's act like grown up American citizens striving for the common good. At the same time, let everyone remember that Rome wasn't built in a day and that age-old customs and traditions cannot be changed overnight.[41]

Another example of active support by a newspaper is this article from *The Tampa Times* of May 27, 1963, forwarded by a contact in that area. The plea for reasonableness and sanity are clearly stated.

---

[40] "Rocky Mount Can Set the Pace," *The Rocky Mount N. C. Telegram* (July 21, 1963), p. 2/3.

[41] "Let's Be Grown Up Citizens," *ibid.* (July 14, 1963), p. 2/3.

A JOB FOR PARENTS OF BOTH RACES

Hillsborough's Superintendent of Schools, J. Crockett Farnell, is wisely preparing the ground now for implementation of a federal court order on integration of students entering the first grade next September.

The U. S. District Court has specified that all children beginning school here next fall, regardless of race, must register at the school nearest them. An alternate choice is provided. A child may be enrolled at the next nearest school occupied predominately by the members of his own race.

Essentially, this means that no student of either race will be forced to attend a school where the majority of students are of the opposite race.

There will be no wholesale integration of Hillsborough's schools under this plan. But there will be some additional mixed classrooms.

Superintendent Farnell has asked parents to cooperate in order that the schools may provide the best possible educational opportunities for the boys and girls involved.

In other words, parental disenchantment with this arrangement should not be permitted to interrupt activities in the classrooms.

We believe Mr. Farnell's plea will win a positive reception. Hillsborough parents are wise enough to recognize that:

—The county has no choice except to follow the court order.

—No student, white or colored, need be penalized by forced attendance at a school whose student body is predominately of the opposite race.

—Demonstrations against the plan will not only be in vain, but they will injure educational opportunities of the children.

This will not be the first integration of Hillsborough classrooms. Ybor City Elementary School has 78 Negro children distributed through all six grades. Negro students also attended Macfarlane Park, Bayside, West Tampa Junior High and Jefferson High School this year.

There is some danger—remote we hope—that racial unrest in other parts of the country may be reflected in local attitudes. That would be tragic. Tampa is not Birmingham. Our own record of interracial accord has been good. There have been differences of opinion and disagreement as to the extent and speed of integrating local schools. The issue was correctly submitted to the courts for an opinion and the opinion now must be accepted as law.

Superintendent Farnell is correct in asking at this early date that parents react intelligently and responsibly to the new plan. Publication of full information now will enable all concerned to study the program and understand its operation. This removes the basis for sudden shock and accompanying emotionalism which too often cancels reason.

Parents, both white and colored, have an opportunity to establish an even firmer foundation for inter-racial harmony here by cooperating with school officials and making a success of this frankly difficult period of readjustment.

The argument is no longer whether we will or will not have integrated classrooms. It is now concerned with making them work in order that children in them get the best possible education and are exposed to the highest possible standards of human relationships.[42]

Factor VI: Residual Support

Factor VI is composed of two variables of statistical significance—desegregated labor unions and school desegregation supported by the state educational agencies.

The Labor Unions

None of the communities which experienced violence had desegregated labor unions. Desegregated labor unions are obvious signs of improved interracial relations and, also, an aid in improving relations by providing a channel of meaningful communication between Negroes and whites.

Since the National Labor Relations Board has ruled "that under the terms of the Taft-Hartley Act a union can be declared guilty of unfair labor practices if it practices racial discrimination," minority groups have a quick and relatively easy means of fighting union bias and eliminating job segregation. This bias caused an NAACP official to declare that "in many instances the unions are worse than management in discriminating against the Negro."[43] Because of this ruling, improvement in employment desegregation is now expected, especially as Negroes become more fully qualified to compete for jobs. Professor Arnold Rose has been quick to point out the importance of education and training as prior requisites to attaining these positions.

Recently, in New York, 700 Negro and Puerto Rican applicants were not even qualified to be interviewed for construction jobs because of a lack of training. In such situations it is clear that legal desegregation of the unions is but one small part in attaining full desegregation of labor unions. An accelerated, cooperative training program instituted by the schools, industry, and government is needed in many areas.

It is interesting to note that, in some cases, Negroes have a better chance of securing a desegregated union job in the South than in the North. In some Southern cities, the percentage of Negro employment in the building trades is twenty times that of New York City.

---

[42] "A Job for Parents of Both Races," *The Tampa Times* (May 27, 1963).

[43] AP quoting Rev. Maurice A. Dawkins in "Integrationists Eye L.A.," *Ithaca Journal* (May 31, 1963), p. 1.

A most notable example of improvement in labor desegregation has occurred in Cleveland and Detroit:

> Negroes have made limited breakthroughs beyond the labor curtain, their gains have been in direct proportion to the amount of political muscle they could show. Detroit's 8,000 member Trade Union Labor Council, an affliate of Randolph's NALC, helped elect the city's mayor, has hammered out agreements with eighteen out of nineteen construction unions calling for admission of Negroes, and runs its own program to train Negro youth for skilled employment.[44]

The correlation between nonviolently desegregated education and desegregated labor is statistically significant in this sample.

State Agencies

The support for nonviolent school desegregation rendered by state educational agencies has varied outlets. Many of the items listed under the favorable role of the state education department in Factor II, the role of the white teachers in Factor IV, and the role of the chief school administrators in Factor I can be aided in implementation by state educational agencies. An example of such action would be the distribution and recommendation of favorable books, articles, and films. Materials disseminated by the agencies might emphasize—

1. an understanding of the nature of civil rights
2. a pride in the past heritage of all groups
3. a sense of common learnings
4. a sense of common service
5. a sense of the spiritual value of each individual[45]

State educational agencies, varying from museums to academic departments, can conceivably initiate and aid in a "low pressure" educational campaign aimed at providing a background of good will and tolerance for the expected school desegregation.

---

[44] Ernest Dunbar, "Black Men White Unions," *Look* (December 17, 1963), p. 44.

[45] Joseph O. Loretan, "Guidelines for Promoting Integration," *Curriculum and Materials,* Spring, 1964, p. 2. Paraphrase of his guidelines.

IV

Final Thoughts

In this study some of the variables significantly related to nonviolent desegregation have been identified. Twenty-three variables have been organized into six factors. Examples for most of the variables have been presented.

It is obvious that important differences in community settings did exist between violent and nonviolent public school desegregation situations. The variables significantly associated with nonviolence in public school desegregations in this study were these:

Factor I: Favorable School Leadership

1. The chief school administrator led in the development of a school desegregation plan.
2. The chief school administrator supported the desegregation plan.
3. The school board supported the desegregation.

Factor II: The Opposition

1. There was a lack of active opposition to school desegregation by the governor.
2. There was a lack of active opposition to school desegregation by outside organizations.
3. There was a lack of active opposition to school desegregation by local organizations.
4. There was a lack of opposition to school desegregation by the state education department.
5. There was a lack of opposition to school desegregation by local individuals.

Factor III: The Urban Center

1. Smaller communities (under 50,000 persons) had better success.

2. There were no Negroes on the police force.*
3. There were no police on duty in plain clothes.*
4. Negro and white schools were comparable.
5. Nearby schools desegregated at the same time.

Factor IV: The Practical Community

1. Desegregation was voluntary (not specifically ordered by a court).
2. There was preparation by the white faculty of white students for nonviolent school desegregation.
3. There were nearby desegregated schools.
4. There was a high employment level among the male, nonwhite population.

Factor V: Active Community Support

1. The white clergy supported school desegregation.
2. Respected white community members supported nonviolent school desegregation.
3. School transportation facilities were desegregated.
4. Local newspapers advocated nonviolent school desegregation.

Factor VI: Residual Support

1. There were desegregated labor unions.
2. The state educational agencies supported school desegregation.

It is evident, on the basis of this broad study of school desegregation, that nonviolence does not simply happen. Careful preparation very often precedes its achievement. There are many factors which provide a favorable social set for nonviolent school desegregation. If a favorable social set is to be provided, many forces and individuals in the community must actively fulfill their responsibilities.

It is equally apparent that nonviolent school desegregation can be attained even if many persons in the community do not favor school desegregation. When it is recognized that the present operational issue is violent vs. nonviolent desegregation, those forces favoring nonviolence can act so as to increase the possibility of achieving this goal. One important step is to identify the forces of active opposition and then act so as to mitigate or control their influences.

The related variables identified in this study would indicate that the burden of social action has a certain specificity. But the implications are that every

---

* Apparently not substantiated by further in-depth probing and thus discounted.

man has an obligation to fulfill. Even in a modern technological society, man is still his brother's keeper.

Some citizens of modern society seem self-condemned to apathy; they think that individual actions don't count or don't matter. Certainly it would be ambitious to seek an answer to that primary question in empirical research. The knowledge that what man becomes is determined by his "turning to the other," by the "I-Thou" relationship of mutuality, and the attempt to provide for the worthwhile needs of one's fellow-man, is gained only through inner experience. For those who do not or cannot look within for these answers, this study may provide a statistical basis for action, may demonstrate the broad responsibilities occasioned by interactions between individuals and groups. The examples of individual action which "did count" may indicate guidelines for the responsible citizen in a community in flux.

In an age when we often take social action on the basis of scientific research, studies like this one are necessary, even essential. But if one asked that all his actions be founded only in science, the consequences would be paralyzing. The combination of scientific method, used in this study, and the inner vision of each individual, vital to the development of the balanced person, is for now the best hope for the individual and the community seeking change with dignity, respect, and cohesion.

APPENDIX A

STATEMENT MADE BEFORE THE CIVIL RIGHTS COMMISSION
BY WILLIAM HENRY OLIVER, SUPERINTENDENT
NASHVILLE CITY SCHOOLS

March 5, 1959

Chairman Hannah and Other Members
of the Commission

Gentlemen:

Your office is aware from previous correspondence that I accepted, with some reluctance, the invitation to appear before this Commission. There are three principle reasons for this reluctance. I should like to state them.

First, and foremost, I feel that any unneccessary airing or publicizing of the desegregation issue in my community at this time is undesirable. The fires of opposition to desegregation in my community have not been extinguished. They are only smoldering. To fan these embers would be foolish, just as it would be foolish to fan the embers under a kettle already still too warm from a flame that has only recently died down. Prudence requires me at the present time to be as quiet as possible.

Second, our case, our plan of desegregation, as you know, is still awaiting judgment in a federal court of appeals. So long as our case is pending in the appellate court, propriety also, I think, would counsel me to be silent.

The third reason may be a selfish one. I am reminded of a soldier who after he had passed through the bloodiest battle of a terrible war came home on furlough and was asked by his friends to tell them about the battle. He replied that he did not wish to talk about it. I feel somewhat the same way regarding some of our experiences with desegregation.

They have been too full of conflict, too much like a battle, for me to wish to talk about them, even though we may have achieved some degree of victory.

All these reasons for my reluctance notwithstanding, however, believing as I do that this Commission is earnestly seeking for truth, and for information which will lead to the most judicious methods of dealing with the momentous and serious problem of desegregation throughout our nation, I am here to speak to you as honestly and frankly as I may concerning our experiences with this problem, and I do so in the hope that what I may say will ultimately be helpful to someone else who may find it necessary to grapple with the same, or a similar, problem. I invite you to ask me any question you please. I shall answer you to the best of my ability.

Before I proceed any further, let me dispel any idea that anyone may have that dealing with the problem of desegregation in the Nashville schools has been a simple or easy, or pleasant task. Nothing could be further from the truth. It has been exceedingly tedious, very painful and terribly difficult. We are thankful that things have worked out as well for us as they have, and we are grateful for what we consider the blessings and guidance of a kind Providence to whom we have constantly prayed and on whom we have steadfastly depended. We are thankful that our children are all in school getting an education, we hope in peace and safety, but we are not bragging. The cost has been too great for this. Since Nashville began to grapple with the problem of desegregation, our most able Superintendent has retired in broken health, his eyesight greatly impaired by pernicious anemia. He was old enough to retire, but he should have been able to retire in good health. The Chairman of our Board of Education, a truly great lady, has suffered a severe heart attack, from which she cannot be expected ever fully to recover, and has had to resign from the Board of Education a year before the expiration of her term of office; and the Chairman of the Instruction Committee, who probably felt more heavily than anyone else the weight of this tremendous problem, has died. Many others among us, including principals, teachers, and other Board members, have suffered in lesser ways, but the memory of long hours of labor, followed by almost sleepless nights, disturbed and harassed by insults and threats by mail, by telephone and in person, remind us that it has not been easy or pleasant. And, if we could forget or ignore these personal things, the pictures remaining in our minds of frightened, terrified children; of disturbed, perplexed parents; of angry, menacing, yelling crowds of misled people; of congested traffic; of glaring headlines in the nation's newspapers; of almost empty classrooms; of a beautiful modern school building blasted by dynamite—these and many other things remind us that the initiation of desegregation in the Nashville schools was not a simple matter. Furthermore, we know that the job is not done. We have only a little more than begun it.

Please believe me when I say that to desegregate the public schools in a city like Nashville is no small matter to be taken lightly or to be dealt with carelessly. Nor can one hope to solve quickly all the problems involved. It will take years—perhaps many years.

What are the principal problems? I should say that the one big problem is that the mixing of the races in the public schools is contrary to the will of a majority of the people. Among some peoples this fact might be of little consequence, but in a community such as ours, it cannot be ignored. It is a part of our idea of government of, by, and for the people that the will of a majority of the citizens in any community should be respected. It has been drilled into our thinking for generations. It seems to us a part of the American way of life. We are accustomed to settling issues by the ballot or through our elected representatives and it is difficult for us to accept a directive from a federal agency in a matter which we regard as being properly under local, or at most state, jurisdiction. Right or wrong, this, I think, is the way the majority of our people think and feel.

It might be helpful for me to describe a bit further, the thinking of our people as I interpret it. Of course, there are some in both races who desire complete integration of the races and who think that this should be accomplished as quickly as possible by whatever means may be necessary. I do not believe, however, that very many Nashvillians of either race hold to this point of view. In my opinion, most of our responsible Negroes simply want to be good citizens just like everyone else. They are not interested, I think, in complete integration, nor do they desire it. They want equal rights, privileges, and opportunities, and equal protection before the law, and who is there to say that they are not entitled to these? But, they do not desire to merge into one mongrel race. Many of our Negro citizens are proud of their heritage and their race, and well they might be.

There are many, very many, people in our community who disagree with the interpretation which the U. S. Supreme Court has given to the Fourteenth Amendment. These are not all just people on the street. They include many professional people, even some of the best legal minds in our city. There are others who contend for what they are pleased to call States Rights, and who feel that this principle has been inexcusably violated by the federal government. There are some who honestly feel that the whole integration issue is Communist-inspired and that behind it is a deliberate effort on the part of our international enemies to confuse and divide the American people. No one can deny that some of the by-products of forced desegregation have been such as would *please* our enemies, for they have caused dissension, violence, hatred and confusion among us. It is equally obvious, however, that the influence of good, sane, level-headed, law-abiding citizens of both races has been strong enough to hold our people and our community together.

I have implied that in the thinking of our people lies our greatest problem. I should like to add that in the thinking of our people lies also the principal *key to the solution* of our problems. Our people, as a whole, stand for law and order. They are opposed to violence. They want an education for their children; and, laying aside in many cases their own personal opinions and disagreements, they have loyally supported their city officials, their police department, their Board of Education and its administrative officers, their teachers and school principals. The respect of the people of Nashville for properly constituted authority, along with their determination that law and order should prevail in their community, has been a beautiful thing to see. If I may say so, I am proud of my people and of our city. The moral support of the good people of Nashville of both races has given encouragement to those of us who have been in positions of responsibility and has enabled us to do our duty. I believe that without their confidence and their prayers, we should have failed utterly.

We have tried to meet the issue of desegregation squarely. There was no way to evade it. We have dealt with our problems seriously, deliberately, sometimes laboriously. We have tried to give a maximum of consideration to the will of our people, especially our parents; we have carried out the directives of the federal court in good faith. We have tried to be honest and fair. We have tried to deal with every individual child and adult according to the principles of human relations laid down by Jesus of Nazareth. We know no better way. We have tried to keep the interests of the *children* foremost in our thinking and in our planning. As to how successful we have been, we leave it to others to judge. At any rate, our children are all in school, and are, we believe, achieving normal success in their studies.

I should like, in conclusion, to emphasize, though I may seem somewhat repetitious, the following points:

1. There needs to be, in my opinion, extensive *background* for desegregation before it should be attempted in a community such as ours. We had this background in Nashville because of the fact that our white and Negro teachers had been working together for a number of years before the U.S. Supreme Court rendered its decision in May, 1954. Furthermore, all our teachers, both white and colored, were on the same basis so far as preparation, experience and salary are concerned. The fact that Nashville is one of the world's leading centers of education and culture for Negroes also helped to provide this background. I am referring particularly to Fisk and Meharry, and to our State Agricultural and Industrial College for Negroes.
2. Following the decision of the Supreme Court in May, 1954, we made a great effort in our school system and in our community to *prepare* for meeting the problem of desegregation. There were numerous conferences involving our principals of both races, our supervisors and our teachers. All our teachers, both white and colored, met together to discuss these problems. We brought in specialists in human relations and we held one in-service training program dealing exclusively with this particular subject.

3. Our Board of Education realized and admitted from the outset that local and state laws must yield to the decisions of the U.S. Supreme Court. There was some disagreement with the decisions of this court, but there was never any question as to whether we were bound to respect these decisions.
4. We had a Board of Education composed of men and women of courage and good judgment who remained at their post under terrific pressure and criticism, resolved to do their duty as they saw it.
5. We had as our Superintendent a man of exceptional educational and administrative stature, a man of integrity, courage and good judgment. I refer to Mr. W. A. Bass, whom I succeeded in office on January 1, 1958.
6. We formulated our plans with exceeding *care*. It was after a tremendous amount of serious consideration that our Board of Education finally decided that the best place to begin desegregation was in the first grade and that the best way to accomplish desegregation of the whole school system was to do it one grade and one year at a time. Even with all our careful planning and with the background which had been established in our community, we had an extremely difficult time when we finally got to the point of permitting Negro children to attend school with white children.
7. We have followed, I think, with *scrupulous honesty* and with a persistent effort to be fair, the plan approved by the District Federal Court for abolishing segregation in our schools. There has never been, so far as I know, any accusation of gerrymandering in our zoning. Most of the job of zoning was done by our principals, with white and colored principals working together.
8. Another most important part of our plan for desegregation is that *parents*, themselves, are given, as far as is reasonably possible within the law, an opportunity to *choose* what they think is best for their own children. I refer to our transfer system. We have granted 100 per cent of the requests for transfer which we have received both from white parents and also from colored parents. We have denied about three requests for re-transfers, but we have granted every single request for original transfer that has come to our office.
9. Our *principals and teachers began* the job of desegregation fully determined that they would be *reasonable* and *fair* and *considerate* toward every child and every parent involved. They have persistently adhered to this resolution and, as yet, I have not had one single complaint from any parents, either white or colored, I believe, as to the way in which our principals and teachers have dealt with the individual students and parents involved. This is a matter of extreme importance and has affected greatly the smoothness and lack of friction with which desegregation has been accomplished up to the present.
10. We had the support of a *loyal police force* and a *strong Mayor* who stood strictly for *law and order*. Without the support of our police department and our Mayor, we could not have established desegregation in our schools. The mobs which made their appearance at the beginning of school in September, 1957, would, in my opinion, have closed down very soon all the schools in our system, one by one, had not our police department established itself as a strong law-enforcement agency. Back of our police department was, of course, our Mayor who can hardly be praised too highly for his steadfast assistance. He was not only involved in the fine work of the police department, but he was also instrumental in helping us to get an injunction through the District Federal Court. Referring further to the *injunction* granted us by the District Federal Court, let me say that this was *an absolute must*. Without it, I doubt that our police department, as fine as it was, could have handled the situation.

11. We had the wholehearted support of local courts. When members of our police department arrested members of the anti-desegregation mob for violence or disorderly conduct or on similar charges, our City Judge assessed penalties with promptness and effectiveness. This was most helpful to us.
12. We had the support of many religious and civic organizations in Nashville, as well as that of private citizens of both races, in our effort to carry out the directives of the Federal Court. Even men who were, in their private thinking, strongly opposed to desegregation supported us wholeheartedly in our effort to maintain law and order and to comply with directives given us by proper legal authority.
13. We had support and assistance from the local press, radio and television agencies. One of our local daily newspapers supported us wholeheartedly. The other could hardly have been said to be altogether wholehearted in its support of our *plan* for desegregation, but both papers strongly opposed violence and lawlessness.
14. We had exceedingly competent and diligent *legal counsel* from the beginning. Mr. Boult and Mr. Hunt are among the best attorneys in our city and, at every turn, we were, I think, most fortunate in the counsel which they gave us and in the manner in which they presented our cause before the courts.
15. I must not overlook the Judge of the District Federal Court. Mr. William Miller. I had not known Judge Miller before our desegregation problems arose and, so far as I know, I have not seen him, even once, outside of Court. I have never had a private, personal conversation with him at any time. I have been deeply impressed, however, with the hearing which he has consistently given to all matters presented in his court on both sides of the desegregation problem. I consider him a Judge worthy of the name, and I think that the thoroughness and fairness with which he has dealt with our problems must not be overlooked.

Finally, what changes would I advocate in our plan if we had to do the job over again? I should say, "None whatsoever." I believe that the plan which we are following is the best that could have been devised for Nashville, Tennessee. I only hope that the appellate court will have the same opinion.

MUSCOGEE COUNTY SCHOOL DISTRICT
Columbus, Georgia

September 16, 1963

A Plan to Desegregate the Schools of the Muscogee County School District, Georgia

I

The Board of Education of the Muscogee County School District, in continuation of its efforts to eliminate, with all deliberate speed, discrimination because of race or color between the pupils of the school district, hereby declares that it will begin to desegregate the schools of the Muscogee County School District by starting in September, 1964, with the twelfth grade, and the Board of Education will desegregate one lower grade each succeeding year until desegregation shall have been accomplished throughout the school district.

II

The Board of Education maintains that the best interests of the citizens of Muscogee County School District will prevail when the Board controls the assignment of pupils to the various school plants and facilities. The Superintendent of Education is hereby directed to continue the maintenance of school attendance areas for each school by keeping a map and word description of each attendance area. The Board of Education will continue its long established policy of assignment of pupils to attendance areas in the Muscogee County School District in order to preserve the orderly process of administering public education.

III

Pupils shall attend the school within the attendance area in which they reside, but transfers, upon the written request of a pupil and his parents or his legal guardian or upon the discretion of the Superintendent of Education, may be made, without regard to race or color, whenever it is in the interest of the pupil or the efficient administration of the Muscogee County School District.

IV

The Board of Education hereby establishes February 1-15, 1964, as the period in which to receive written applications from pupils and parents or legal guardians for transfers and reassignments to the twelfth grade of a high school other than the one to which the pupil is currently assigned in the Muscogee County School District. The written applications setting forth reasons for transfers and reassignments will be evaluated and either approved or disapproved by the Superintendent of Education no later than March 15, 1964, and written notice mailed to parents at the address shown on written application no later than ten days after the decision by the Superintendent of Education. The pupil and parents or legal guardian may appeal in writing the decision of the Superintendent of Education no later than the regular April meeting of the Board of Education. The final decision of the Board of Education will be made no later than May 1, 1964, and the pupil and parents or legal guardian will be given written notice at the address shown on written application of the decision by the Board of Education within fifteen days.

V

The Board of Education will consider written applications for transfers and reassignments for new pupils moving into the school district after February 15, 1964, no later than August 1, 1964. All pupils must accept the original assignment to the school within the attendance area in which the pupil resides, but will be permitted to file written application for transfer and reassignment to the twelfth grade of another school by the Superintendent of Education.

VI

All newcomers moving into the Muscogee County School District after August 1, 1964, must register and attend the school in the attendance area in which they reside, but may file written application with the Superintendent of Education for transfer and reassignment to the twelfth grade of another school. Such written applications will be processed as expeditiously as possible by the Superintendent of Education.

VII

All hardship cases, upon written application and full explanation of the facts in the case, will be given full and sympathetic consideration by the Superintendent of Education and the Board of Education.

VIII

In the administration of this plan the Superintendent of Education is directed to take into consideration all criteria that may affect the best interest and welfare of the pupils and the efficient administration of public education in the Muscogee County School District, but no consideration shall be given to the race or color of any pupil.

IX

The same procedure for filing written applications for transfers and reassignments and approving or disapproving such written applications for transfers and reassignments will prevail in 1965 and each year thereafter as outlined for the school year beginning September, 1964.

X

The Board of Education, in its discretion, may revise, change, or amend these rules and regulations or any one of them.

THE ATLANTA DESEGREGATION STORY: A SYNOPSIS

The story of Atlanta's desegregation of four high schools in the early fall of 1961 is a chronicle of good people with strong prejudices who changed their minds when given the facts without emotion, who chose the high road when faced with valid alternatives, and who emerged to dignity and wisdom when the testing time came.

It is the story of a kaleidoscope of variegated emotional patterns which dissolved and reformed: indifference to consternation, frustration to defiance, futility to facts, knowledge to understanding, and rationality to wisdom. And self-respect.

It is the story of astute and courageous leadership by public officials, of unremitting and responsible presentation of all the facts by the press, of dispassionate and free discussion of issues by religious and lay organizations, of a hardnosed, no-foolishness attitude on the part of the police department.

It is the story of a series of developments in both the national and local scene from whose dialectics emerged one pitiless piece of logic: Comply with the law or perish in catastrophic ignorance. Atlanta chose to comply—with dignity, and then with a peculiar pride.

And, finally, it is the story of a plan for the opening days of school, conceived by the administrative staff of the schools and executed, under the scrutiny of the police department, with a meticulosity of detail characterizing the D-Day landings. The crank, the crackpot, the lunatic fringe—homegrown and imported—didn't have an opportunity, not a prayer of a chance, to be himself. For a few days at least he was a model citizen.

When the Supreme Court spoke its fateful words in 1954, the man-on-the-street greeted the pronunciamento with masterly calm. The reaction, if any, was "It can't happen here."

In January, 1958, Atlanta Negroes, in a class-action suit in the Federal Court sought to enjoin the Atlanta Board of Education against the practice of racial discrimation. In June, 1959, the bench ruled in favor of the plaintiffs and ordered the Board to submit a plan of desegregation by the following December. But the Atlanta Board of Education could not submit a plan of desegregation without running counter to Georgia's massive resistance laws which automatically forced closure upon any school or school system admitting a single Negro to a white school.

At this point, resistance to integration was so irrational that even school people and ministers scarcely dared to advocate the continuance of public education.

But voices of reason began to be heard in the land. In November, 1958, the Atlanta League of Voters, after a delineation of the ethical and legal issues by Ralph McGill of the Atlanta Constitution, sponsored an open meeting to discuss ways and means of keeping schools open. The climate of opinion was such that the steering committee felt a public declaration in favor of open schools would be undesirable and premature.

At this time the man-on-the-street desisted from castigating the Supreme Court, the damyankees, the Communists and the do-gooders only long enough to sputter "Never! Never! Better no schools at all."

In December, 1958, less than a score of white parents chartered HOPE (Help Our Public Education). This organization took no position about integration or segregation. The members committed themselves, however, to the unqualified objective of open schools. By March, 1959, an open-schools movement had spread to other large towns throughout Georgia.

Meantime, well-financed and well-organized opposition had taken form in the States Rights Council, the Klans, the White Citizens Councils.

In late November, 1959, the Atlanta Board of Education submitted a reverse stairstep plan of desegregation, beginning with the 12th grade and proceeding a grade a year until all grades would be desegregated. This plan was approved by the Federal Court in January, 1960. Since the plan was headed for an unavoidable collision with State laws requiring school closure, pressure mounted to repeal state massive resistance laws. But there was no outward sign of change except that an appointed legislative and citizens committee, which came to be known as the Sibley Committee, conducted public hearings throughout the state to assess public sentiment about closing schools. The hearings were televised and widely publicized. The hearings brought out two important points: the issues became finely drawn; there was a strong sentiment throughout the state for schools to remain open even at the cost of integration. This latter development profoundly impressed the politicians who have a preternaturally keen ear for noises which may reverberate in the ballot box.

The man-on-the-street or lounging on the courthouse steps was thinking straighter now. And he wrestled with a decision which was ultimately inevitable because he was basically sensible.

In May, 1960, the Federal Court stayed integration of schools for one year, declaring that the integration plan would become effective in the fall of 1961 "whether or not the General Assembly of Georgia at its session in January 1961 passes permissive legislation." The Georgia Legislature was given one last chance to prevent closing of the schools by abolishing massive resistance laws.

By the fall of 1960, advocates of open schools engaged themselves in widespread activity to avoid the impending clash between Federal and state laws. These individuals and groups included important religious bodies, business leaders, lawyer groups, educators, and civic organizations. Forums and discussions throughout the state allowed the possibility that integration was inevitable if schools were to remain open; further, the conclusion often reached was that schools must remain open, come what may.

Concurrent with the opening of the 1961 Georgia Legislature in January, a crisis developed at the University of Georgia. Two Negroes had been ordered admitted to the state university. The probability of closing the University of Georgia caused dismay and revulsion. Disorder and near-rioting were permitted to climax entry of the two Negroes at Georgia. State officials hesitated to close the university where many legislators were alumni, and where their sons and daughters and those of their neighbors now attended. Governor Vandiver, in a dramatic reversal of position, offered a "Child Protection Plan," accepted by the legislature, which in effect nullified existing school closure laws and permitted certain face-saving provisions to die-hard communities.

The battle for the principle of open schools had been won.

Atlanta school officials proceeded to execute the provisions of the pupil placement plan whereby applications were to be received and processed from Negro students desiring to transfer to the 11th and 12th grades of white high schools. Briefly, these procedures were as follows:

1. Application of Negro students for transfer, under provisions of the placement plan
2. Consideration of factors of scholastic aptitude and academic achievement, and of proximity of residence to requested school
3. Interview and decision

From about 300 picking up applications, some 133 Negro students actually submitted requests for transfers. Of the 133, 48 were selected for further testing and 17 for interviews. Finally, 10 students, outstanding in academic ability and achievement as well as traits of personality and character, were selected for transfer to four white high schools. Throughout these procedures, the press and other news media were kept fully informed. These media handled developments and facts responsibly and factually.

In the summer of 1961 an organization called OASIS (Organizations Assisting Schools in September) was formed to create a climate of calm, dignified compliance with the law. These organizations comprised church, business, service, and youth groups of the community. OASIS sponsored or stimulated hundreds of meetings. This phase of developing a public opinion receptive to compliance with the law was regarded as a key to desegregation when schools opened on August 28.

The administrative staff, after consultation with the police department and community leaders, formulated a detailed plan covering all phases and aspects of school life in the opening days. Newspaper men and representatives of the news media, parents and non-school people generally, and, in fact, all persons except students and teachers were strictly barred from school premises and from the streets adjacent to the school grounds. Parking on school property or in the vicinity of the school was banned except in the case of teachers holding parking cards. Traffic was tightly controlled. Loitering was forbidden. Parents could deposit their children at the school but were required to move on. Delivery of the Negro transferees was accomplished by Negro city police in civilian clothing whose movements and deliveries were carefully staged and exactly timed. All parents of students in the four desegregated schools were informed by a letter from the principal about all aspects and regulations concerned with the opening of school.

Relationships with the press and the other news media deserve special mention.

The Superintendent, with substantial help from the mayor, provided a central location for receiving and transmitting all the events and possibly newsworthy developments. This concept proved to be both practical and fascinating from the viewpoint of the news agencies. The Council Chambers at the City Hall were converted into a vast press room. Ticker tapes, a dozen television sets beamed at the four high schools, direct radio contact with these schools, and an open and amplified two-way telephone communications installation provided reporters with more complete and accurate coverage of news and developments than a ringside seat at any one of the schools. Fried chicken, coca colas, and ham sandwiches were served at no cost. The Superintendent and mayor, as well as other city officials and personages, circulated freely among the newsmen and were available with comments and observations. Principals of the four high schools were interviewed periodically by direct-line, amplified intercommunication system. Representatives of the newsgathering agencies were cooperative and grateful. Their articles and news reports fully reflected their gratitude and were characterized by responsibility and fairness. It was indeed a fruitful public relations project.

What factors were most effective in creating a climate of acceptance? At the risk of oversimplifying a complex situation, the following seem paramount:

1. The Atlanta Board of Education had sought by all legal means to avoid integrating the schools. The Board was not regarded as "integrationists," "race-mixers," or "communists." Hence, when the Board announced its intention to desegregate, the feeling was general that the Board had exhausted the legal possibilities of maintaining segregation.
2. The mayor, the police department, and the newspapers consistently took positions of moderation and, when necessary, spoke in favor of continued open schools, with integration if necessary. The mayor was nearing retirement age but he was a colorful, wise, and astute politician with a popular following and a long record of efficient city management. The newspapers were responsible and pitiless in their exposition of the facts. The chief of police was hard-boiled, practical, and incorruptible.
3. The evolving and developing pattern of court decisions elsewhere in the South was presented in the newspapers with interpretation and full implications. The intelligent had only to read the history elsewhere to predict the outcome here.
4. The crisis at the University of Georgia precipitated an impasse in an area where the governor and legislature were emotionally vulnerable. Come what may, the University of Georgia would not be closed. This climax, antedating the Atlanta crisis, was a fortuitous prelude.
5. An important factor was the vast reservoir of people in Atlanta (a) who were committed to fairness and justice to all the citizens on the basis of Christian and democratic principles, (b) who were fearful of interrupting the economic progress of the city and state, (c) who were knowledgeable politically and sophisticated generally, and (d) who were basically decent, law abiding citizens.
6. Lastly, the Board, the administration, and the teaching staffs exercised proper timing in their move from apparent apathy to strong and courageous leadership. It was neither precipitant nor laggard. It acted when action could be effective. In leadership, and in the specific detailing of plans and operations, the Board of Education and the administrative staff were characterized by the guile of a ward-heeler and the idealism of a missionary. It was a wedding of practicality and idealism.

To tell the story of desegregation in Atlanta is to trace the development of a people—certainly including students—to a new maturity and a new sensitivity. Perhaps it was fitting that Wesley Pittman, a senior in desegregated Henry Grady High School, should somehow capture the essence of the enlarged conception of human dignity in the following poem which he titled "I Know You" and which appeared in the school paper:

Hey, wait a minute, dark skinned boy. Do I know you?
Some would turn away, and hurry on.
But somehow I've got a feeling that I know you.

I know your eyes, and your easy smile of teeth flashing white and happy. I know your laugh which starts within and rises to the surface, like bubbles in a clear blue lake.

Your grandmother raised my father, and he knew her gentle love, and her humble Godlike grace.

I've walked across dew wet fields with your brothers, have seen the tall stalks of corn awaken with the wan rays of early light. And we listened to the mockingbirds, and felt a special feeling.

I know your kindness, your goodness—not your darkness. For what is skin but a thin membranous covering? Why, nothing else at all. Each of us has his blackness, and each his white.

Hey, do I know you, dark skinned boy?
Why sure, by all that's true I do!
I've worked and played and laughed with you.
I've sung your songs, told your stories.
I've fought for my country beside you, in a muddy ditch.
I've smoked a cigarette with you, and shared a joke or two.
I've known God's earth and life with you, rejoiced with you, been sad with you.
Of all the millions of lost and forgotten faces, you remain.
Hey, wait a minute, dark skinned boy—
I know you, I know you.

BREVARD, NORTH CAROLINA

Transylvania County is located some 50 miles southwest of Mars Hill. Brevard is the county seat. Comparatively speaking, this is a small county—approximately 16,500 population. Up until a few years ago, agriculture, lumber and small business supported the economic structure of this community. Today, we still have some farming, a little lumber—pulpwood, etc. However, basically the county is now industrial—Olin Industries, DuPont E I DeNemours and Company, Inc., and several other small industries complete the economic structure.

This change from agriculture to industry brought about tremendous changes in the lives of the people of Transylvania County. Today, after 25 years, there are still elements of resentment over the change caused by industry in a rural community. Even after you have been in this community for 20 years, you are still a newcomer.

Last fall we moved into another area of social change. Social change that is going to be much more lasting and upsetting than the change from agriculture to industry. I have been asked to give you the procedure taken in Transylvania County for the integration of schools. It's somewhat like a fat lady caught in a revolving door—there is no way out without considerable trouble! It's about as frustrating as the man I heard about in Washington—"Doors. Men-Women. Colored-White. Protestant-Catholic. Republican-Democrat."

From 1948 to 1963, the negro high school students of Transylvania County attended school in the Hendersonville City System. This fact alone placed Transylvania County in a most vulnerable position. Some 70 negro students were being transported 20 miles to a school in another county.

For eight years we heard very little discontent among the negro people. During this time we had several requests, mostly from white ministers, to form committees and study the problem. The Board did not approve the formation of such committees. Committees of this type can be of some value if carefully selected and given good guidance in the job they are to do. Otherwise, they may create certain obligations without responsibility.

On May 5, 1962, the Board of Education received a petition from six negro parents requesting that all negro pupils be reassigned to the schools in Transylvania County. This petition was turned down on the grounds that the six signers of the petition did not have the authority to request re-assignment of school children other than their own.

Following this action, the six negroes signing the petition asked for a public hearing. This was granted. Some thirty negro families appeared at this hearing.

The speaker for the group stated their case. Listing carefully the reasons for requesting the transfer and re-assignment, the Board of Education took no action at that time. Later in an executive session, the Board again turned down the request by the negroes for the assignment of all colored children to the schools of Transylvania County. The parties concerned were notified by registered mail of this decision. This action was reported in the local newspaper and on the local radio in order that the public might be informed of the procedure being followed by the Board.

The next step was individual letters from negro parents requesting that their child or children be assigned to a specific school. . . in this case, either the Junior High or the Senior High. Each application was given careful consideration. There were better than 40 individual applications. From this group 8 negro students were selected for re-assignment—2 in each grade level 9-12. These students were selected as a cross section from the most outstanding student to the low average. Of course, those not re-assigned took exception to the decision and asked for a hearing on the matter. A series of public hearings was set. The negro plaintiffs were represented by Ruben Daily; the Board of Education by Ralph Ramsey, Jr. The Board again refused the request for reassignment. The above described action took place between May, 1962 and March, 1963.

In the meantime, 7 or 8 pupils assigned to Brevard Senior High and Brevard Junior High had satisfactorily and quietly adjusted along with the white population in their respective schools. This was done without a visitor or phone call from the public. This, I think, was due to the feeling of the public that the Board had carefully considered all possibilities in arriving at its final decision.

Of those pupils assigned, one passed all work taken. The other 6 failed from 1 to 4 subjects. This will probably be one of the more difficult problems in the transition of pupils.

On May 11, 1963, the Board of Education and Superintendent were served a subpoena to appear in District Court before Judge Warlick. As the defendant we asked that the case be dismissed. This was overruled. We further asked that action be dismissed against the County Superintendent of Schools and members of the defendant Board in their individual capacities. This was granted.

The court granted the plaintiffs' prayer for relief in that the defendant Board was enjoined from refusing solely on the basis of race or color to admit, enroll and educate the minor plaintiffs in the Brevard Junior High School and The Brevard

Senior High School, and from assigning the minor plaintiffs to public senior high school and public junior high school outside of Transylvania County, North Carolina.

The court did not rule on elementary schools or staff.

As of this date some 70 pupils of the colored race have been assigned. This constitutes the total negro high school pupil population. Further, there is no indication that the people of Transylvania County have not accepted this decision as final.

To summarize, I would say:

1. A definite plan should be set and followed.
2. The Board of Education is the legal representative of the schools and should make all decisions affecting the schools.
3. All decisions by the Board should be firm, and well-thought out; not based on street opinions.
4. Decisions should show loyalty to the social patterns of the community—yet common sense in the face of the inevitable.
5. Publicity should cover only the facts, and should not be made into a fiction story for the public.
6. All individuals should be treated with respect and dignity and all proceedings kept very official.
7. Once the decision is made and the transition of pupils has been accomplished, no exceptions or rule changes should take place in the individual schools. All students should be treated alike, having the same privileges and responsibilities.
8. Above all, select the best legal counsel available to advise you in your procedure.

ALABAMA COUNCIL ON HUMAN RELATIONS
Birmingham, Alabama

An address, "Citizen and State", by Dr. Marion A. Wright, Linville Falls, N. C. before a joint meeting of Alabama and Georgia Councils on Human Relations at a workshop in Tuskegee, Alabama, October 4, 1963.

This is an important occasion in Southern history and, incidentally, in my own experience. For the first time two State Councils on Human Relations hold a joint meeting. For the first time in my life I have two sponsors—something like being presented by B. C. and Anacin. I select those two because I am sure your organizations have your headaches—"have you tried B. C., B. C., B. C.?"—and need occasionally to *control* yourselves. Probably it is the misery which loves company which brings you together.

I certainly hope that, before this memorable meeting, the coach of the Georgia Council didn't call up the coach of the Alabama Council and give away secret information about Georgia's defensive formations. (Our councils, of course, are always on the defensive.) But, if such a conversation took place, we hope the Saturday Evening Post gets the story. What couldn't we do with $3,000,000!

Not only is the occasion unique. So is the place of meeting. Tuskegee has many claims to distinction. I could, perhaps, ingratiate myself with you by reciting them. (I am not above a little ingratiating.) But, because it fits in with my purpose, I limit myself to only one of Tuskegee's badges of distinction. Probably that one has appealed to me because I know one of the participants in a drama which had its setting in this city. In this way I have the warmly satisfying feeling of involvement with great events. This is much like the O'Henry character who was always bragging that his grandfather had been kicked by General Lee's mule.

Anyhow, this Institute's Dean Gomillion and I were both born in Johnston, South Carolina—I will not say when. We both left in early youth. Probably 40 years elapsed before we saw each other again, by which time I had failed to get an A. B. degree and he was a Ph.D. dean of this institution. Now, wherever I go, I run into him or find his pug marks. He is a constant reminder to me that, if I had settled down, and learned my geometry and Latin and all that junk, I, too might have become a dean or something.

But what interests us now is not C. G. Gomillion, Dean, but C. G. Gomillion, plaintiff, in the case of Gomillion vs Lightfoot. His career is further proof of the fact that a really able and dedicated man can find ways to serve his country—ways not connected with the things he fitted himself to do. Mr. Gomillion no doubt worked hard and long to become a professor and dean, both of which roles he fills with great distinction. He never worked a day to become a plaintiff in a law suit. As an old time fellow citizen of mine, he will not, I hope, mind my saying that long after he is gone to wherever good deans go, and has been forgotten for all of his fine work here, lawyers and judges will read and ponder what he did in the unfamiliar field of the law. His name is emblazoned in the reports and in the moving volume entitled *Gomillion vs Lightfoot.*

Now, I didn't go into all of this merely to pay a deserved tribute to an old friend, though I have satisfaction in so doing. I did it as an indirect and somewhat sneaky way of getting us to think together about certain matters.

At one of these I have already hinted. It is that, above and beyond a man's career or profession, and infinitely more important than they, is his role as a citizen. We are too apt to stereotype people. This man is a lawyer, a doctor, or a dean, or a farmer, or a musician, we are told. Instantly, if subconsciously, we call up an image and decide the man must be of a certain type. We label him and file him away under his appropriate heading. This is, of course, pre-judgment, which is merely a polite term for prejudice. Others, when told that a man is Protestant or Catholic, Jew or Gentile, Chinaman, or white or Negro, leap to their own hasty conclusions and exalt or condemn without hearing. Such is prejudice in its baldest form. Of it we in Alabama and Georgia have tragic knowledge.

One's career as citizen is a thing apart from all such extraneous considerations. Society is properly concerned with none of these. Gomillion as citizen is a more important and heroic individual than Gomillion as dean. Who cares that George Washington was a surveyor, or Ben Franklin a printer, or Tom Paine a maker of corsets? They might have cared one time about Tom Paine's specialty but, from examining the ads, I don't believe they would now. The thing with which society is concerned is whether or not a man pulls his weight, pays his way, as a citizen. To do less than that is a form of parasitism.

But that is not the real point I had in mind about *Gomillion vs Lightfoot.* The point is that the case which originated here is not merely a landmark of the law. It gives every decent and law-abiding American hope for his country's future. It illustrates what Chief Justice Warren had in mind when he said "Law floats in a sea of morals." The case represents the conscious effort of the law to bring itself into accord with sound morality.

You recall the facts—the legislative re-drafting of this city's boundary lines into a geographical monstrosity for the purpose of disfranchising a large percentage of the population. The court has always had extreme reluctance to interfere in cases of gerrymandering, indulging every presumption in favor of legislative honesty and good intent. But there are limits to the presumption. The decision is a ringing affimation that public morality will not be forever sacrificed on the altar of sterile legalism.

In another connection Alabama drove the court to the same position. The pupil placement law was at first upheld upon the ground that, if fairly administered, pupils would be properly assigned to schools. There was again the presumption of honesty and good intent. But the discreditable and ignoble use made of the statute forced the court to step in and correct abuses. This was the triumph of morality over form.

And, if we may pursue the point a little farther, the celebrated *Plessy vs Ferguson* case established the separate-but-equal-doctrine. Implicit is the court's trust in legislative and administrative honesty. But experience demonstrated the contrary—always separate, never equal. There was an essential immorality in application of the principle. So the principle was reversed in the 1954 Brown decision.

It has become a popular sport among Southern politicians to sneer at "the Warren Court". There will come a time—indeed it is here in the rest of the country—when men will give devout thanks that, at this juncture in history, there emerged and functioned a court which responded to the claims of sound public morality. And, if there are those disposed to believe that no good thing can come out of Nazareth, let them reflect that Birmingham and Alabama, which produced Governor Wallace, produced also Justice Hugo Black.

A man named Gerry gave his name to create the term gerrymandering, a synonym for using strictly legal means to accomplish an immoral result in geographical subdivisions. I suggest a synonym for using legal means to secure moral results in the same field. The word is Gomillionizing.

The point of all this seems to be that, if you want your cause to succeed, be sure it is grounded in morals. It is not enough to assert the moral position sporadically and only in times of crisis. That is what is now taking place all over the South. What is required is a day to day and issue by issue assertion of the moral position. We should never cease proclaiming: Segregation is morally indefensible —in the school, in the park, in the lunch counter, in the picture show, everywhere, and especially in the church. Cato concluded every oration "Carthago delenda est" —Carthage must be destroyed. Voltaire ended every letter "Escrasez l'infame"—Crush the infamy. We must exhibit the same daily resolution.

"Law floats in a sea of morals." The councils on human relations should permit no haziness to exist anywhere on the point that there is a moral force in the community which not merely condemns violence (certainly zero in indignation) but insists as a matter of common decency that in every public facility all are treated alike. When we sharply define the moral issue, we influence and forecast the legal decision. Thus we throw our weight around.

Let us be as precise as possible. What are some moral issues to be defined? Perhaps all of us would come up with different answers. But since the theme of this meeting is "New Ways for New Days", I shall plunge in with my own version. I hope it is no mere sense of the dramatic which prompts me to strike at the jugular. Anyhow, I propose that we should meet the State's Rights argument head-on and expose it for the fraud it is.

No one here, I am sure, is fooled by the State's Rights cry. When funds are being handed out in Washington we never hear it. Post offices, federal buildings and installations of all kinds, crop subsidies, erosion control money, aid for hospitals and all the rest—our representatives are there, passing around the hat and rushing into print to proclaim "Look what I got for you". No taint on the money, no fear of federal control, no cry of State's Rights. Only when a Negro citizen asserts a constitutional right—to vote, to attend school, to use a park, to dine in decent surroundings—only then is the cry raised in the land, only then are we warned against "outside interference in local affairs".

It is the instrumentalities which quickly transport and convey men, goods, and opinion, rather than any formal paper agreement, which have made this one nation, indivisible. (The segregationist needs occasionally to be reminded that the rest of the quotation is *not* "With liberty and justice for *some*.") When the nation became actually one and indivisible, justice also became indivisible and could not be measured by different scales of values. So, the segregationist's quarrel is not, as he supposes, with the NAACP, President Kennedy and the Warren Court; it is with MacAdam, Henry Ford and Marconi.

Since states and communities do impinge upon each other and since the experiments they conduct affect for good or ill their neighbors in other states and indeed, the entire nation, the national government is forced to have a concern with what goes on within these once insulated cells. If Prince Edward County wishes to experiment with bringing up a generation of ignorant boys and girls, and if Alabama and Mississippi wish to experiment with a system by which Negro citizens are barred from attendance upon their state universities, the government of the United States would fail in the national duty if it did not put an end to these poisonous adventures.

So, if local practices present a national danger, they invite the use of national power to bring them to an end. We must bear in mind also that the citizens upon whom these experiments are conducted are citizens, not merely of a state, but of the United States, and, as such, entitled to national protection.

We must extract such comfort as we can from the conduct of wicked men. So let us give thanks to Senator Byrd, to Governor Faubus, to Governor Barnett, to Governor Wallace. What the senator did in Prince Edward County and what the governors did in Arkansas, in Mississippi and in Alabama awoke the country into a realization that these were no mere side shows to which the nation could remain blind and indifferent. Those incidents affected *American* citizens entitled to *national* protection. They were of profound *national* concern. If Mississippi and Alabama won't protect American citizens, the federal government will.

We have moved into a new day. This country will never be the same after the grisly events which took place in Little Rock, in Oxford, in Birmingham. The methods of the police state, long unrebuked, now stage their final orgy. No state has the right to suppress, to intimidate, to disfranchise. A citizen is entitled to enjoy in Alabama and Mississippi rights enjoyed in Massachusetts or Wisconsin.

So the Southern governors have forced a re-consideration of the relationship between the states and the federal government. They did much more than that. They have forced you and me, as citizens, to re-consider our relationship to society. We move into a new day. The old relationships do not suffice.

The church is an institution of society. Can we any longer give sanction, support or membership to a segregated church? The cruelest of all injuries is inflicted by the one agency which claims some divine or supernatural authorship. To turn one away from a lunch counter is evil; to turn him away from the altar is diabolical. What distinction is there in principle between boycotting or picketing a place of business and boycotting or picketing a place or worship?

When a minister is fired because he advocates welcoming all who would worship, is it enough to say "tut, tut" and settle back comfortably into a pew? Seven theological professors at Sewanee some years ago resigned in protest of exclusion of a Negro student. That action changed the institution's policy.

When we wink at tokenism in assignment of pupils do we not endorse token morality and is our own morality quite robust? One woman, Mrs. Jessie Daniel Ames, personally carrying resolutions and petitions of women to reluctant sheriffs, almost alone drove lynching out of the South. In this new day has not the time arrived when committees of resolute women may by personal appearance before school boards bring an end to the scourge and hyprocrisy of tokenism?

When proprietors of businesses exclude Negroes or discriminate against them, personal visits from disturbed and concerned white persons may be effective supplements to the picket lines.

Boys and girls are in jail for going into forbidden rest rooms or singing hymns on State house steps. Can we not visit and cheer them and sit with them in court? We no longer dare to be squeamish or be moved by considerations of distaste.

At many places in the South parks, play grounds and swimming pools are being closed. These are instruments of civilization. Their closing is a retreat from civilization, an advance toward savagery. No good citizen can view that action with complacency. Every member of a state council, and the councils themselves, to the extent permitted by their tax exempt privilege, should not go unprotesting back to the Dark Ages. Surely it is legitimate to print the arguments which originally inspired the establishments of these civic ornaments.

Many years ago, when Dr. Frank Graham was president of the University of North Carolina, a faculty member went over to Durham and dined with a Negro. There was a movement among the trustees to fire the professor. Dr. Graham announced "If you fire him you have my resignation." That ended the movement and set the stage for the University's later gracious acceptance of Negro students. By such individual acts of private citizens does a state secure deserved fame and honor.

By contrast, James Reston in the New York Times, gives names of twelve powerful citizens of Birmingham who might have averted that city's shame. They were mute when they should have spoken. One is reminded of what Hesiod wrote in 720 B.C.: "Often hath a whole city reaped the evil fruit of one bad man." That was 2700 years before Bull Connor!

And Marcellenus, still B.C., wrote: "He that would live completely happy must before all things belong to a country that is of fair report."

So, by a very roundabout way, we come again to *Gomillion vs Lightfoot.* A private citizen confronting the power of a state. But the conflict was not as unequal as one might think. Dr. Gomillion chose the battleground, as the Greeks chose Thermopylae and Salamis, where they were strong and the enemy weak. He chose to fight on a moral issue. There he was at home and Alabama was on unfamiliar ground. He was strong and Alabama weak. Any state, steeped in immoral policy cloaked with legalism, is inevitably vulnerable to attack by a private citizen whose cause is just. And, by making his stand, the citizen educates the state in basic morality. In the same way he may educate his church in basic religion. And society in basic humanity.

The tragic events which have occurred in Birmingham will have taught the South nothing if they result only in search for a scapegoat, one who will "bear upon him all our iniquities into a land not inhabited", as the Biblical phrase has it. Certainly the search is not difficult. There abound in many quarters in the South mean and ignoble spirits, who, from governors' offices and legislative halls, by calculated words and deeds, have inspired stupid and brutal men to barbaric acts.

But, if we are to seek for first causes, these political figures are themselves mere creations. Their words receive attention and their acts have authority only because they occupy the pedestal of office. We, the voters, placed them there, "drest them in a little brief authority", and so gave them forum and power. We begin to pay in flame and blood for our folly.

Too often those who "strut and fret their hour upon the stage" have had accomplices of surface respectability—irresponsible elements of press and bar, the White Citizens Councils, and in some instances, the pulpit. The press by urging resistance; the bar, by devising evasive schemes and interposing fictitious defenses, and the pulpit, by giving ecclesiastical sanction to segregation—all set in motion forces which came to flower in a charred church and four small graves.

The list might be indefinitely extended. There are in every state a company of accessories to the murders, bombings, assaults, intimidations, repressions and lesser crimes which stain Southern annals. Sneers about the "Warren Court"; endless prating about "our Southern way of life"; the cries of "nigger lover"; the tattered and vulgar jokes about Negroes and the accompanying thigh-slapping and guffawa; the vote to turn them out if they come to our church; the ostentatious change of seats in bus or plane if the next seat is occupied by a dark-skinned person; the sneer and the scowl, designed to put them in their place—all of these and much more known to every Southerner have helped to create the soil and climate in which our prize crop of demagogues has thrived. These are activities of those positively, if unconsciously, involved in setting the stage for thugs with bombs.

But, paradoxically, the most seriously involved offenders have been the uninvolved. They are the persons of anemic decency, "the meanly wise and feebly good", who have sat out this social revolution. They were not active parties to the dishonorable evasive maneuvers which preceded violence; they had no hand in their state's pretension to compliance with law while actually defying it; they were not massive resisters or token integrationists; they initiated no policy of exclusion of Negroes from church membership or swimming pools or golf courses. Nothing overt can be laid at their doors. But they are guilty of the monstrous sin of uninvolvement, of benevolent neutrality, of disengagement from the struggle which raged about them. They had weight and power which were not used. Evil succeeds when good men do nothing. Not to participate in a crucial moral conflict may insure a whole skin which houses a craven heart.

Justice Holmes said; "I think that, as life is action and passion, it is required of a man that he should share the passion and action of his time at peril of being judged not to have lived."

How many of us have failed to share the passion and action of our times!

Shall Birmingham's lamented and tragically dead have died in vain? If we go back to business as usual; if we engage in legalistic arguments over the right to expel a customer; if we resume the petty school tokenism which means also moral tokenism; if gradualism is still our shibboleth—the sacrifice shall have little availed. But if, at last, shocked and contrite, we marshal the region's moral resources, if the white South will match the Negro's courage and nobility, we shall emerge from the Birmingham horror, cleansed, purged and dedicated to the creation of a more nearly perfect society.

In their death four little girls may lead the South into a more abundant life.

FLORIDA AND SOUTH GEORGIA INSTITUTE FOR SUPERINTENDENTS AND BOARD MEMBERS ON THE CIVIL RIGHTS ACT OF 1964

February 24-26, 1965

Dr. Samuel Ersoff, Dr. Michael J. Stolee, Co-Directors, School of Education, University of Miami, Coral Gables, Florida, Under a Grant from the United States Office of Education.

Introduction

An institute for Florida and South Georgia School Board members and superintendents was held at the University of Miami during February 24-26, 1965. The purpose of the institute was to help these important school officials understand the provisions of the Civil Rights Act of 1964 as it affects education and to gain ideas on how best to comply with this act. A grant from the U.S. Office of Education to the School of Education made the institute possible.

Outstanding speakers were featured on the program. In addition, panels of superintendents, principals, board members, Florida and Georgia State Department of Education personnel, and lay resource people discussed their experiences and answered questions about school desegregation plans. Representatives from the U. S. Office of Education and from the U.S. Commission on Civil Rights also participated. All in all, an attempt was made to provide points of view from various sizes, types, and levels of schools, communities, and agencies.

Insofar as possible all the sessions were recorded on tape. Herein is presented a report of the proceedings as they developed from day to day. While this report has been edited for the sake of brevity, nothing has been done to alter the meaning or the ideas conveyed. Wherever possible, the exact words of the speaker have been transcribed.

After the program is listed, the actual day by day events are developed. The remarks of the featured speakers are included in the exact part of the program in which they were heard.

Also included are evaluations made by the participants. These were obtained on the last day of the institute and were the results of an evaluation sheet which was distributed at the time.

Dr. A. F. Tuttle, Associate Dean, Stetson University, was originally scheduled to present his evaluation before the group on Friday afternoon, February 26. Due to a change in the program he was unable to do this. His intended remarks are included in this report. Finally, a listing of the participants, is found.

We are pleased to submit this report. We should like to extend our sincere appreciation to all those who participated in the institute. We feel that this type of program is necessary to develop an exchange of ideas, points of view, and information for such a vital issue. Only by bringing these out into the open can the channels of communication be improved and progress made.

The School of Education of the University of Miami was most pleased to serve as host to such a distinguished gathering and to such a worthy cause.

Samuel Ersoff, *Co-Director*

Michael J. Stolee, *Co-Director*

Negroes are eligible for membership in the F.E.A. I think some are maintaining dual membership, some in the integrated organization and some in the Negro organization. I think it is reasonable to assume that in two or three years, as soon as we get staff integration in the two groups, we will only have one group in Florida. Of course, the big problem in this is that we do not necessarily want to have one follow the other and that's the thing that worries Negroes. Integration is not integration if it is fusing out the Negro schools and the Negro activities.

Probably the greatest help we have had in recognizing some of the problems we faced was the influx of Cubans. That gave us a flexibility of curriculum so that we were able to adjust to this total problem. Maybe the idea that we cannot teach people, that we can't get enough levels or enough tracks to take care of various levels of people have been emphasized through this whole social change and maybe we are going to start in teaching individuals. I know that we are more flexible in Dade County now than we were five years ago. Everyone of these people here has a multiple track program. You can do almost anything you want to within that program to meet the needs of youngsters. When you get a group of youngsters, you could start working with them. And that is true in schools that are not integrated too. It has been a healthy thing for our total curriculum development program in my judgment.

All of us and all of you are afraid to ever use the personal pronoun, we. I guess in this whole area, all you'd ever know for sure is what I think and I am not always sure of that. When I say "we" I don't know whether I was speaking for anybody besides me or not.

This is an area of education, of social change, where I believe that educational leadership is going to have to work out and develop followship that is willing to move along these lines. As far as I am concerned, when we develop a good educational program to meet the needs of the various youngsters within our schools and to meet the needs of the community, in many cases it results in a school program that will operate 14, 15, and 16 hours a day. We, therefore, have the community school program going on where another person comes in the afternoon at 1:00 o'clock and goes through to 10:00 o'clock at night with a variety of community activities. Maybe we would come to the conclusion that the school is not the only educational institution in the world that affects children. We might have to go back and take off our sophisticated high hats and recognize the fact that in reality this is a total job we have with a total community that affects boys and girls and we can't ignore the adults and the other influences in the community and make it a total educational program. Certainly we can't draw a line between general education and adult vocational education and somehow or other make it a total program to take care of that community. We've enjoyed being with you people. We've enjoyed having you in Dade County.

Dr. Ersoff:

I would like to thank the members of this fine panel for the excellent job which they did here this morning. I think you have seen exemplified in the personalities of Mr. Matthews, Mrs. Ratcliffe, Mr. Lupoli, Mr. Burroughs and Mr. Stradley the kind of educational leadership which is typical of Dade County and which we feel has made this one of the finest school systems in the country. They haven't tried to tell you how to do things, they merely share with you their experiences and their reactions to the things which have happened to them.

Thursday Afternoon, February 25, 1965

Dr. Stolee:

Mr. J. Mac Barber tells me that the Georgia Senate has passed the appropriations bill yesterday and it might come up to the House this afternoon or tomorrow. He also tells me that the House Rules Committee is about ready to pass out the Reapportionment bill. So, tomorrow morning, we are hoping yet for Mr. J. Mac Barber, but if he is not here, you understand there are important things going on in Atlanta and Mr. Halligan will be here instead.

There's been another program change. We had originally scheduled small group discussions to be held tomorrow morning at 10:45. We have found that you have a lot of questions that could be answered only by Mr. Dave Seeley, who was an assistant to the United States Commissioner of Education and is now the Director of the Equal Educational Opportunities Branch. Instead of our small groups talking about methods of developing acceptable plans, he is going to tell us what he will be looking for. We thought this would be of value to you.

They weren't able to get any airplanes off the ground this morning up in Jacksonville. This means that Dean Kimball Wiles of the University of Florida can't make it. But I am happy to say that we've prevailed upon Dr. Robert Myers, who is Associate Professor of Education at the University of Florida, to chair that panel in his place.

We have as our speaker a man who can tell us many things about our problem with a great deal of insight. Our speaker was born and brought up in Birmingham, Alabama. He went to college at Tuskegee Institute in Alabama. He got his Master of Arts degree from Fisk University, Doctor of Philosophy degree from the Washington State University and has done post doctoral work at the University of Connecticut. He has published approximately 25 articles in learned journals dealing with the general area of race relations. Several months ago, I went to the principal of one of our schools here in Dade County, and I asked, "If you were to pick one person whom you would like to address a group of superintendents and board members and who would do the best possible job of presenting some thought provoking ideas and explaining some ideas to them, whom would you choose?" It didn't take him more than a second to say, "I would choose Dr. Charles U. Smith, chairman of the Department of Sociology at Florida A. & M. University." I am happy to present to you Dr. Charles U. Smith.

Dr. Smith:

Dr. Ersoff, Dr. Stolee, Superintendents of Education, Members of School Boards, Ladies and Gentlemen: I am pleased and honored to have been asked to speak to you at this Institute. I congratulate the University of Miami and the immediate sponsors of this Institute for their foresight in what may well be among the guiding lights for approaching educational problems on the contemporary American scene, and especially in the southeastern region. For while the problems of the contemporary educational scene in America are relatively new and complex and require originality and creativity in their solution, they were not unanticipated by social scientists and thoughtful laymen. Events occurring many years ago and trends emerging over a substantial period of time (which cannot be chronicled here because of time limitations) resulted in a pattern of continuity leading inevitably to the problems and possibilities of education in America today. Thus war, depression, poverty, industrialization, urbanization, modern developments in transportation and communication, increased literacy, and scientific knowledge have, over the years, provided a seedbed from which judicial decisions, legislative action and social policy have emerged providing us with the problem under consideration at this Institute; namely, how can modern public education successfully and effectively deal with the problem of desegregation?

In order to have a fuller appreciation of the nature of the desegregation problem in public education and especially how it affects the Negro student in the desegrated situation it seems desirable to review briefly the nature of culture and its transmission and distribution in America; and more specifically, the subculture which has molded Negro students now venturing into the process of desegregation. Against such background a description of how the desegregation process affects the Negro student should be more clearly discernible; and educational policies and programs to deal with the problem may be more rationally conceived.

Briefly, culture may be thought of as all of learned behavior and the products of learned behavior, socially developed, and transmitted from one generation to another. Thus culture includes non-material traits, complex in pattern, such as language, customs, laws, values, folkways and moral beliefs; as well as material elements such as tools, buildings, machinery, artifacts, clothing, etc. It would seem that in a democratic society such as America the total content of culture would be accessible to all individuals either as a matter or right or personal effort and achievement. The fact is, however, that although the culture content of American society is universal in its reality a number of other factors prevent the total content of culture from being equally acquired by all members of the society.

Within one's geographic region, community, neighborhood, family, and peer group certain aspects of the total culture may be selected for emphasis or attention at the expense of culture traits which may be regarded as being of more value in other parts of the society. Furthermore, in a particular region, community, or neighborhood, certain individuals and groups may be prohibited from participating in the same way in various aspects of the culture. By way of illustration of this point we may refer to the fact that the South has through the years selected certain racial values from the total culture content of America; has given these values a certain emphasis, and consequently has systematically restricted the activities of the Negro, as well as the point of view and activity of the white southerner.

Regardless of the aspect of culture selected by a particular local area or grouping, the interpretations of these culture elements may, and does, vary from group to group and community to community. By interpretation, I mean the way in which the particular culture trait or pattern is meaningfully made manifest and operational in a region, community or family. For example, in the South racial segregation has been traditionally selected as a social pattern. But the interpretation of segregation has historically varied from place to place and group to group within the region. Thus one community in north Florida has customarily permitted Negroes to hire taxicabs with white drivers while 50 miles to the east such would not have been tolerated. In certain parts of the South segregation has included persons standing in lines at banks and liquor stores while such a degree of separation has not been thought to be necessary in other parts of the South.

Thus, when the culture trait or pattern finally reaches the individual it may bear little resemblance to the national conception of it. The result of this reduction and modification process of generalized culture patterns by localized groupings is what the sociologist refers to as *subculture*. And in the final analysis it is the subculture that surrounds an individual which provides his perception, action norms, and definitions of situations. It becomes clear, then, that when an individual or group is impelled to action with regard to some situation, the action taken is very likely to be in accordance with local subcultural norms rather than the more generalized ideal of the society as a whole or the subcultural norms of an unfamiliar grouping or remote geographic area. What is real, proper, logical, and sound to a person is very largely determined by his subcultural environment. The subculture, therefore, is extremely significant in the child's state of preparedness for learning at the time of entry into school, the child's self-conception, his level of aspiration, his motivation, as well as his overall appreciation of the educational process and its goals. The content and goals of modern public education in America for the most part have been established by native, white, Protestant, gentile, urban, big city, middle-class, males. The student who possesses the greater number of these background characteristics is more likely to succeed in school. On the other hand a foreign-born, Negro, Jewish, rural, farm, lower class, female will be more likely to fail in school. And the probability of failure should increase in proportion to the number of these latter traits possessed.

Let us now turn to a brief examination of the subculture of the Negro so that we may have a fuller knowledge of the typical Negro student entering the desegregated educational system.

First, the subculture of the Negro has been, and still is, one of restriction and frustration. The Negro is still generally confined to traditional roles and jobs—largely because of prejudice and discrimination–but also because his subcultural experience has left him ill-equipped to take advantage of emerging opportunities in the desegregated economic and social structure. The Negro is, perhaps, the only minority group in America that enters the occupational hierarchy at the top and bottom at the same time. He is forced to take a job at the lowest level and, for him, that is as high as he can go. (e.g. working on the garbage truck—rarely gets in the driver's seat.) In the State Capitol at Tallahassee, Negroes begin work as janitors and retire from this same position 25 years later—they are never upgraded even to clerk or the euphemistic sanitary engineer.

The Negro is further frustrated by the repeated admonition by well-meaning whites that one must "earn" his civil rights. Seventy years ago, Booker T. Washington was naive enough to believe that if Negroes proved themselves to be good craftsmen and hard working deserving citizens that their full acceptance by whites would be automatically forthcoming. The years from then to the present time have forcibly demonstrated the error of this thinking.

The Negro wonders how the Hungarian refugees of 1959 "earned" their civil rights in America. Or how the Cubans expatriated from their native land "earned" theirs. Here in Miami, Cubans not only have rights and jobs never permitted the Negro but also have taken over many of the traditional Negro jobs (e.g. waiters and bellmen on Miami Beach). The Negro is required to take baths, pass intelligence tests, earn high degrees and develop super skills before he can begin to go first class.

Second, the Negro's subculture is a world of fear, anxiety and suspicion. The Negro has to be fearful and anxious about things beneath the perception threshold of whites. He is forced by experience to anticipate insults by police, waiters, elected officials, and white supremacists. He has anxiety as to whether or not he will be able to eat in a restaurant, sleep in a motel, urinate in a restroom, or fish or swim in the international waters of the Atlantic Ocean. He is forced to be suspicious of whites who refuse to pay the minimum wage, who induce him to sign contracts which he cannot read and interpret correctly, who sell worthless insurance policies, who sell him Cadillacs and color television sets by day and burn crosses before his home by night; and who shoot into his car as he drives, without stopping, through a town.

Third, the subculture of the Negro is a subculture of poverty and illiteracy. The poverty I speak of is well below the standard set by the Economic Opportunity Act. As a matter of fact, if many Negro families had incomes of $2999 per year they would feel that they were living rather comfortably. The poverty I speak of is the grinding enervating poverty of the three-room, unpainted shack, with a water faucet —if any—in the yard, or on the back stoop; usually without electricity, and no inside toilet. I can find many examples of this in Tallahassee, other Florida cities, and those of south Georgia.

The illiteracy of the Negro is too well known to belabor here. The subculture of the Negro neither required nor permitted the development of widespread appreciation of literacy. And most literate Negroes have less than two generations of literate ancestors behind them.

Fourth, as Silberman says in his *Crisis in Black and White*, the subculture of the Negro is a subculture of "inferiority." By almost every criterion known to man,

Negroes in general do not measure up to whites. Test scores, income and wealth levels, life expectancy, health status, cultural exposure, political prominence and accumulation of power show that Negroes are lower than whites. (There are exceptions—Thank God for Bob Hayes, Wilt the Stilt, Willie Mays, Jimmy Brown and Cassius, the Greatest.) And this inferiority is often reinforced in Negro youth by school teachers and administrators complaining of their "poor" background, low aspiration and stultified motivation. Teachers and schools often resort to "social promotion" to move the problem along rather than eliminate it. The Negroes' self esteem must suffer under these circumstances.

Fifth, the subculture of the Negro, especially as related to education, has been a subculture of accommodation and apathy—one wherein the goals of the school were not goals of education, but rather, the goals of segregation—thereby inducing accommodation to routine, and nondescript and unimaginative curricula, and apathy about the achievement of high standards in teaching and learning. Substantial evidence can be marshalled to indicate that principals and often highly ranked instructional personnel achieved their positions because of demonstrated willingness to accept the status quo in the education of Negroes and/or demonstrated ability to maintain "smooth operation" within the segregated school and to preserve overt "racial peace and harmony." In the Negro schools the overriding goal became that of "not rocking the boat" of racial segregation. Except for mechanical salary increments and continuing contracts relatively few Negro school personnel felt the need, or were encouraged to obtain higher competencies for educational purposes in their chosen fields. Such persons having vested interests in the protective wall of segregation have become increasingly anxious about their futures as desegregation became more imminent and their capabilities and performances might be exposed in the hard cold light of comparison with their white counterparts. While this pathetic situation exists, in fairness it must be pointed out that such persons are largely products of the segregated subculture of the Negro, externally imposed by white superiors.

From such a system could only emerge students possessing attitudes of accommodation and apathy toward educational excellence and the essentiality of learning.

Psychologists, social psychologists and sociologists have amassed bodies of evidence to indicate that Negro children growing up in this subculture often tend to have attitudes of self-hatred, authoritarianism, submission and deference, negativism toward learning, and hostility, even toward the segregated Negro school. Since the school—even the Negro school—espouses concepts not congruent with other aspects of his subculture, such as emphasis on literacy, it therefore is often visualized by the Negro youth as an enemy to be fought or avoided. Hence, truancy, vandalism, and dropouts.

What happens when a child or youth from this subculture finds himself voluntarily or otherwise in the desegregated school, most often with a predominance of whites? How does desegregation affect the academic performance of Negroes? Irwin Katz has reviewed and evaluated the greater portion of the empirical evidence on this problem (*American Psychologist*, June, 1964) and most of the comments that follow are based on this article.

Negro students who pioneered the desegregation process as specific litigants in Little Rock, St. Louis, and the like, are not typical of the Negro student population since they were carefully selected as "guinea pigs" on the basis of superior academic performance. School systems now facing the problem of desegregation will, in all probability, have to deal with increasing numbers of more typical products of the Negro subculture.

Social threat is one fear that the Negro child in the desegregated situation is likely to experience. Social threat refers to the anxious expectation that others will inflict harm or pain. While in many instances of desegregation few overt attacks on Negroes have been manifest because of his conditioning in his subculture where suspicion of whites is pervasive, the Negro students often carry the burden of this threat —whether real or imagined. Such threat will obviously be unfavorable to his scholastic performance.

Social rejection and isolation of the Negro child by his white peers in school may be a significant factor in the lowered performance of Negroes. Evidence indicates that Negroes in desegregated situations fear disapproval of whites and often have covert or internalized symptoms of distress, such as enuresis, nightmares, withdrawal and pathological physical symptoms. Other evidence indicates that in schools where social acceptance was typical, academic success was achieved. (Jas. Meredith never accepted; Hamilton Holmes—never studied in the library, ate in a dining hall, used the gymnasium, entered the snack bar, visited no whites and were visited by none.)

Another class of factors tending to be detrimental to the performance of Negroes in desegregated situations is *probability of success*. The evidence indicates that Negro students have feelings of intellectual inferiority which arise from an awareness of actual differences in racial achievement, or from irrational acceptance of the white stereotype of Negroes. Studies demonstrate overwhelmingly that education in Negro schools is inferior to that of whites. This fact has been widely publicized. Desegregated Negro students, knowing this, may not even try hard to succeed or excel, believing it impossible. Other evidence suggests that Negro students often perform more poorly on tasks after being told that they are competing with whites. Thus, the belief of Negro students in the low probability of success when in competition with whites would tend to reduce effort.

Finally, *failure threat* is another class of stimulus events which tends to reduce effort. This is the feeling that harm, pain, or disapproval will result as a consequence of failure. The pathological consequences of this type of threat may result from the fear of sterotyping of all Negroes by whites as a result of his failure, or from the feeling that he has "embarrassed" the Negro race by failing. Negroes in desegregated situations still feel that they are "representing their people"—a feeling all too often reinforced by well-meaning white teachers and administrators. (e.g. you are a "credit" or "disgrace" to your race!)

Finally, ladies and gentlemen, one point remains to be touched on. What should educational administrators and policy-makers do to facilitate the process of school desegregation?

1. Take a positive attitude. In those instances where the duly constituted officials have assumed a positive and optimistic posture the desegregation process has proceeded with a relative minimum of trauma.
2. Don't lower standards. The Negro student does not want the school and teachers to emulate his deprived subculture, and be like him.
3. Organize campaigns to develop pride in school learning and intellectual achievement among Negroes.
4. Procure funds and establish effective programs of compensatory education for Negroes (e.g. Higher Horizons, the Great Cities Project) to bridge the gap between the subculture of Negroes, and the required culture of educational achievement.
5. Identify the positive aspects of the Negro subculture and utilize these in educational programming.
6. Avoid unconscious prejudice and inadvertent discrimination e.g., "your people."

7. Develop in-service programs to aid teachers to perform better in the desegregated school.
8. Procure scholarship and grant funds for Negro teachers so that they may go to school, obtain better qualifications and thereby compete on a more equitable basis for positions in the desegregated system.
9. Learn to accept Negro adults as peers and to deal with them on this plane. Plan "with" them and not "for" them. Avoid paternalism.
10. Marshal the creative and imaginative talent that opposed desegregation so successfully for so long and use its ingenuity in facilitating the process.
11. Institute programs for contacting the parents of Negro students and help them to understand what they can do to prepare children for school and to foster achievement once the children are in school.
12. Reassess the predictive value of conventional tests as indicators of the achievement of Negroes in light of subcultural conditioning, and new empirical findings.
13. Utilize all appropriate provisions of the Civil Rights Act and the Equal Opportunity Act in facilitating the school desegregation process.
14. Provide for the extension of interracial contacts of students, parents and educational personnel beyond the school setting, so that Negroes and whites may learn to be at ease with one another.
15. Utilize proportionately more textbooks, library materials and institutional aids by, and about, Negroes in the normal routine of school.

Finally, I submit, that these things should, and must be done; not because I say so; not to comply with either court decisions or the Civil Rights Act; but rather to take one giant step toward the realization of the American Ideal and our democratic way of life.

Dr. Stolee:

Dr. Smith, thank you. You know he's getting to be quite a frequent visitor at our campus. Maybe one of these days, we will get him away from A. & M.

I am happy to introduce to you the moderator of the next panel, Dr. Bob Myers, Associate Professor of Education at the University of Florida.

Dr. Myers:

Thank you, Mike.

This afternoon we have a panel addressed to the proposition of looking at school desegregation and resulting community understanding or misunderstanding. To keep it at a scholarly level, they have chosen as the four panel members scholars in the social sciences. You have just heard Dr. Smith, sociologist, from Florida A. & M., and next to him is Mr. Virgil Pitstick, Assistant Professor of Human Relations here at the University of Miami. Next to me here on my left, Mr. Larry Knowles, Professor of Law at the University of Louisville, who among other things, has worked with the federal government on civil rights legal aspects. On my left, Dean H. Franklin Williams, Dean of the University College at the University of Miami.

Now our procedure this afternoon for this panel is going to be a bit different. We're going to hear from each of these men with the exception of Dr. Smith, who said he has made his charge and will skip this five to ten minute presentation. Then we're going to discuss among ourselves some of the things that have been said and then we are going to throw it open to you for your questions, so shall we start now with Dean Williams:

Dean Williams:

I hope you won't mind if I begin by saying I am an historian by training and I have been read out of the college professors because I am tainted with administration as a dean, but I think I should tell you that my administration duties have for some years included the title Director of Community Affairs, which I gave up a year or so ago.

As Director of Community Affairs, I was expected to have contact with organized groups in the community and these included not only United Fund groups, religious groups of various kinds, but also a multitude of community organizations. Miami is blessed with a large number of organizations which are interested in the problems of community organization. We have a Welfare Planning Council which deals with social welfare problems, we have an Anti-Defamation League, an American Jewish Committee, and an American Jewish Congress, The National Conference of Christians and Jews, and we have a number of similar organizations that are devoted to bettering human relations in the community. The result is, sometimes, a considerable division of effort and conflict but it also affects the pattern of the community. That community is not a typical community, anyway. We are so far south that we come back on the other side and are perhaps a Yankee outpost down here.

What I'd like to talk about is my picture of what I have seen in this county. You've heard about it, I understand, from the side of the school system. In the 1950's I was working with a community organization, the Dade County Council on Community Relations, which was established after a couple of unpleasant bombings of a synagogue. This was supposed to be, if it had worked out as we hoped, a partially governmental, partially voluntary organization that would try to bring about a better understanding between groups. Those who worked with it had in mind the possibility already apparent at that time that there might be a decision with regard to desegregation of schools. Those cases were pending. And they felt that perhaps we ought to do some preparatory work in the community. I participated in a number of panels, in which we attempted to bring to P.T.A. groups and the like the idea that desegregation had occurred. We had some examples from New Jersey, one from Indiana, and one from Texas that we used as illustrations. What we had in mind was that minds needed to be open, so that they would accept the fact when it came. One of the interesting aspects was that we did some good in the sense of bringing public acceptance but the sad part is no one can measure it and I don't know whether we really affected the situation at all.

The decision finally did come and one of the interesting moments to me came within a few days of the decision when this group had a breakfast with the Attorney General of the State of Florida. At that time, I feel we "missed the boat" in this area because the mood of that meeting which did reach some of the power structure was suggested by the Attorney General's remark "The decision is on the books; since we will have to carry it out, we might as well plan on how." We felt very much encouraged, those of us who had been facing this possibility.

But then came the failure to move and the delay, the repeated court cases, the final prosecution of a particular case for Florida. During that interval some of us hoped to establish contact with the school board and the school administration and a few informal contacts were made but there was a failure to communicate. I remember one occasion when we had a long session and came up with the conclusion from the school administration that they had no plan, because they refused to discuss any plan until there was a decision and they could justify it by a court decision. At this time, the school board would not tell an outside group what it was planning and we felt very much frustrated.

The second contribution I may be able to make is a little story from the experience of the University of Miami. The University of Miami was never officially segregated, but in practice it was. There was no real provision for segregation and, as a matter of fact, for some years before the decision to desegregate, the University taught a good many Negro students but it taught them on a segregated basis, had classes in the Negro high schools where University credits were duly entered for them for transfer to other institutions where the degrees might be obtained. There were also a few other cases of non-credit courses that were desegregated. In a number of other areas we had a degree of desegregation in terms of interest. For an example, a question would come, "If a Negro music teacher wants to come to the faculty concert of our music school, how about it?" We applied the measure that if the purpose was one that was natural, such as a music teacher wanting to hear a concert, we would allow them to come. On that basis the symphony orchestra had Negro subscribers.

Finally in 1961, the board made the decision that from that time on admissions to the University of Miami would be without regard to race or religion. The decision was made just after the February class had registered and so in effect, we had one semester's notice before we had to act on this decision. During the period a committee was appointed and it was my privilege to sit on this committee and I look back on it with great interest because we held a meeting and asked "What are going to be the problems?" First, we had to decide if the board really meant what it said. Did it mean that we'd admit them and then treat them differently and we decided, no, that wasn't what it meant. If we admitted them on an equal basis it really was a commitment to equal treatment.

Then we began to say, "Well, where are the problems going to come from?" And from each department of the University there came a really fascinating array of problems. Of course, there was the problem that if you allow admissions, are you going to allow access to the dormitories? Are you going to allow complete access to the Student Club? And then the farther reaches of the planning began coming in. How are you going to handle it when you have teacher interns going out into the community and put a Negro into a white school or a white intern in a Negro school? Everybody had problems. I can remember we had an agenda that was four or five pages thick.

We were still trying to decide what we were going to do in September when it suddenly dawned on us that summer school was coming up and a great many Negro teachers were going to take advantage of the pronouncement. Finally after laying out a few basic lines, we said, "Let's see what happens in the summer and then we may know." The only thing that happened was a few complaints from Negroes that they weren't given enough attention because they were treated like ordinary students and they really thought they were pioneers in a way and perhaps they ought to have been made over a little, but this was our policy. We have never, for an example, made a formal account of how many Negroes we have. We know it's not very many because of the economic factor involved. With a $1200 tuition for an academic year, you are out of the bracket of many Negroes as I think Dr. Smith will recognize readily enough. During the next few months, it was interesting to me that we kept coming back, "Do we really mean that we're going all the way in treating a Negro student like the other?" We had to convince ourselves several times over that, "Yes, this is what we meant." There never was any real trouble.

I want to tell you just one more thing about this. We said at the start that what we do on campus is our business. We will not say what has to be done outside. We couldn't really stick with that because our students felt that this was not enough. Increasingly we began to find evidence of some sort of activist movement among our students, primarily our white students, at the failure of stores and restaurants in the neighborhood to receive Negro students. This took the form of an action before our Publication Board to propose that the University's newspaper should refuse advertisements from restaurants which had segregated practices. We took this to the board and the board voted that in logic, you had to do this. The board divided on this and some student opinion resisted. They said you had to let them advertise anyway. But the vast majority of us felt that when a firm advertised in a student newspaper, it invited all students to come and we were not willing to be a party to the psychological trauma that might result if the student were then refused. We expected community reaction to this. We notified all advertisers that they would have to accept this practice. It went off without a tremor, but there was a little complaining from one or two places. We lost one or two advertising accounts that had been rather easy for the business managers to collect over the years but after about three months, one of these came back to us and asked "Will it be all right if I say that I will receive any University student?" We said "That's all we can ask." It wasn't our business whether he received the Negro community other than students and he came back and so far as I know, his advertising was accepted.

Two things I think are lessons from this. We were helped in community acceptance by the fact there was never any question of the firmness of our decision. The second thing was that the problems tended to be worse in anticipation than they were when we got up to them.

Dr. Myers:

Thank you, Dean. Now, Mr. Knowles:

Mr. Knowles:

I was at the Gainesville meeting with many of you. There, in terms of getting the job done, the mechanic's action, "What have we got to do and how do we do it?" was settled with plea to do good and avoid evil. I suggest that this fairly definite plan doesn't work. You're going to have to do something else, and I am speaking unofficially now. In the tactics of desegregating the first thing you can do is simply to zone geographically, lock everybody in, allow no switching schools and end it there. But you will get the tradition of the Negro school and you can't lock a white kid in a traditionally Negro school. Change the name to the Robert E. Lee and paint it, but at least start thinking in terms of changing the old look, the old customs. If you have two schools right beside each other, a Negro and a white school, each with grades one to six, why not make one of them one to three and the other four to six.

You are going to have to face faculty desegregation, too. You're going to have to start thinking about it today and not tomorrow because the sooner you think about it, the better off you'll be. How do you desegregate a faculty? These are some of the things that have been done. Here's one; the first thing you do is take a Negro teacher and make her a librarian. She's not in front of a class, she doesn't have the sensitivity reaction of the hard core and nobody phones up. Another thing you can do is to make her a special service teacher; music or gym where she meets with the kids one hour a day, not all day. This is just realizing the facts of life. We have to figure out the community worries and how they are going to react. Next step, reversed faculty desegregation.

How do you take a white teacher and put him in an all Negro school or the formerly Negro school? Well, the first thing you do, don't put one in there, put three or four. Make one fellow the principal or an assistant principal, if you want. To the young people coming into the system, you say "Look, if you want to train for administration you are going to have to be exposed to all the cultures in the communities. Consequently, you're going to have to go to a Negro school and teach there for a year. If you're going to adminster the school system you have to be familiar with the school system." Put a block of teachers in. Take three Negro teachers out of the Negro school and put three white teachers in, not one.

Another thing you could do it in the special education class. Put a Negro teacher there or a white teacher in vocational education with the mentally deprived, the slower learner or underachievers. These people will not complain. If the child is in a special education class, the parent is not going to complain that a Negro teacher is helping that child learn how to read. If you say, "Well, Negro teachers are inferior," then the next step is to keep all Negro teachers in a Negro school. Then who is getting the unilaterally inferior education? If you start using these assumptions you're going to have to work them all the way.

This is not the termination of faculty desegregation, but this is the beginning.

Dr. Myers:

Any one of the panel wish to react, raise a question, direct a question to any of the members of the panel? Dr. Smith, you haven't had a chance to speak.

Dr. Smith:

Well, I don't know whether I want to react to what anyone else has said. Someone raised a question this morning and I don't know whether I can answer it, about where is the Negro leadership or who is the Negro leadership? Another professor from Florida State University trying to identify changes in Negro leadership in one community found that the traditional concepts of leadership in the community and the Negro community have to be altered in many areas now. We found, for an example, in this community that we studied in a period of about six or seven years the leadership changed completely with a possible exception of one or two individuals who were able to make the switch from what we call the old leaders to the new leaders.

In general, it appears from my own study that the new leadership is the so-called militant leadership, that the older tactics of leadership are not generally acceptable to the Negro community any more. We found, also, there was tremendous reluctance on the part of officials in the white community to be willing to deal with the persons they regarded as rabble-rousers, agitators, and so on. The older leaders were unable to deliver any more. I suppose the final test is whether or not they can deliver the kinds of things that you have been accustomed to their delivering. Can they commit the Negro community or at least a sizable portion of the community to any particular proposition with the people following them? This was not true in the community that we studied.

Often we find that people make a mistake of assuming that a leading Negro citizen is a leader of Negroes. This may be the case, but all too often it isn't. The most prominent Negro physician in the community, the most prominent businessman may be the people who are most powerless in the whole struggle for civil rights and all too often they are the ones who are distrusted. A prominent Negro business man, for example, may be distrusted because people feel that he has notes and mortgages at banks and other obligations which would tend to tie his hands and he is not free to act as he would like to. Oft times, the Negro physician has his practice built up because of segregation. They rarely have white patients and so segregation is really making their medical practice grow and so they do not feel that they should "Rock the boat" and destroy the little empire they have built. So, you have to be very careful about the desegregation process.

In trying to establish an articulation among the members of the community, it is very important to maintain an open mind. Simply because you resent the activities of a person does not mean that person is not a leader, and does not mean that person is unintelligent. I know that it will be distasteful many times because many of these "New Negroes" violate the traditional codes that we are accustomed to. They are not nearly as courteous as we would like them to be. They don't say "yes sir" and "no sir" and yet these are the people who really in many communities have the power.

I think I can say without violating the law that from time to time I do a little work with the Community Relations Service in Washington. All this work is confidential, but very recently I've run into this situation and I think we were able to convince members of the community that even though you don't like to deal with these people, it is unfortunate sometimes that the representatives of SNCC and CORE and all these other organizations don't really look like we would like them to look. They will wear beards, goatees, and fuzzy hats, sweat shirts and they go in lumbering boots and sometimes you may think they need a bath but these, very often, are the ones to which the community responds. They do not respond nearly so often to the Negro principal. As Mrs. Ratcliffe pointed out this morning, the Negro principal and most of the Negro teachers are in a difficult position. They are not free and even if they did act on the basis of principle, a lot of times they are not trusted by the lay members of the community because they feel that their hands are tied. I just mention this as one of the aspects or one of the factors that needs to be carefully understood and carefully studied if we want to effectuate better community understanding in this whole process.

Dean Williams:

I'd like to ask Dr. Smith how a well-intentioned white group seeking to meet that leadership can find it. I have been sitting on a board where they said, "Let's get Negro leadership to share with us." The first names that came up I recognized as the previous generation of leadership, a couple of school teachers, a doctor and a dentist who had been identified with the political leadership with the Negro community, but I still did not know enough to say for certain who the next generation of leaders were. How can we establish communication to get at the real leaders?

Dr. Smith:

Again, this is a very difficult question and I might say that also in Tallahassee, as someone indicated this morning, we tried to find the real leaders in the white community. We've always felt there was a hidden power structure there; that the city commissioners and the city officials were really spokesmen rather than policy makers. We have never been able to document this. We feel that we could really name in Tallahassee ten or twelve prominent white families who, if they would say something about a particular issue or speak up, would soon decide a matter of policy. They never do. We could never prove it, so we don't know.

So trying to identify the real leaders in the Negro community is equally as difficult, perhaps more so because few of them are in elected positions. I would say, and this really won't answer your question, that you have to judge by the results of the people, well, the followership really. If they call for a demonstration, do they get anybody? If they have a public meeting, does anyone come? We've been very much concerned in our community about Negro voting and registration and for years we've been concerned and for years we've been trying to get people out to register and we've hauled them in buses and hauled them in cars and we still never get more than about 60 per cent of the Negroes registered.

About a month ago I happened to be talking with a person who lived in another part of town, and she began to tell me about people who were regarded as leaders, not necessarily militant, but leaders in various other aspects of the community. I didn't know or never thought of the leaders in the large movement. Large is tremendously important to Negroes. I ended up with a list of 40 people, only about five of whom I had any real knowledge of. I haven't had a chance to test this to see whether they really can produce voter registrants or potential registrants, but the fact was that here was a person living and having grown up with some of these people who was able to produce a list this long of people whom she felt would be influential in any kind of city undertaking.

The only thing I can suggest is that you may need to talk to some different people instead of talking to the people that you know who might suggest leaders. Why not talk to a waiter some time in a restaurant, talk to the head bellman at a hotel if he happens to be Negro. I'm not saying they will always give you valid leaders because oft times, you know, bellman and waiters have been accused of being "Uncle Toms." This is not always the case. Some of them are among the most militant people that we have. But see if by contacting diverse groups or representatives of diverse groups, you begin to get a sort of piling up of names and people agree that if you go to 15 organizations of people from 15 different occupations and socio-economic levels and you begin to get the same names over and over, it's very likely that among these are persons who are regarded as the leaders in the Negro community.

Dr. Myers:

I'd like to comment just briefly on some of the things we do know about community power structure. According to Hunter, you have three levels of membership in power structure. There is the top level, decision makers or as it was called yesterday, gate keepers. This is very small select group. In a small community of 10,000 people, it may consist of four or six people, maybe ten or twelve in a larger community. One the size of Miami would probably have subpower groups in various areas, because it would be more complex in a larger city. These people are not easy to know. They do not hold public office generally.

The second level is the implementing level. These are the people who put into action the decisions that are made by the top power key. These are the presidents of the Rotary Clubs, the people whose names are frequently in the paper, the people who organize communities for the Heart Fund, the United Fund and are the ones who implement decisions as made by the top power key.

Then you have a third level. These are called the runners. These are the people who carry "the word to Garcia," so to speak. These are the ones that make certain the plan is implemented after it's been decided upon. This can consist of 100 to 200 people. They are the ones who are in the know. You find them up and down Main street. Usually they do a lot of talking, but generally they take their orders from others.

Kimbrough has recently done a study of community power structure as related to education. He has never found in his studies nor have we been able to discover where a superintendent of schools was a member of the top power. Now, we haven't been able to find where the officials in schools, principals and teachers were even on the implementing level. We have found superintendents who were runners and principals who were runners. We wouldn't have such a problem as we're facing and studying here for three days, if all of us were members of the top level of the power structure. We would just go back and say, "Here is our decision," and we'd do it. We all know that we aren't members of the top power level of the local power structure. But the membership of this has to be known.

I have a question from the floor on the power structure. Undoubtedly these top people, decision makers, decide whether or not this is going to affect them and some of our studies show that in some communities as many as 80 per cent of the things that come along, they just let happen. But when it gets close to their vested interests, then they come forward with their decision. These people are basically good people, and they're thinking what's best for their community. They are not despots. They are not people who take delight in hurting people or ruining people's lives. This is their image of the community and what it ought to be like and they want to pass it on as a stable good community. So, frequently, they will not take any stand at all.

I'm following up your question whether there is a club to which the members of the power structure will belong where by informal communication they will reach a consensus?

Yes, we found that they do meet and they clear things with each other. It's an informal group organization with very strong norms, very strong goals, purposes, and rules of conduct.

Dr. Smith:

If I understand you correctly, this is exactly what the situation was. I would say about 10-15 years ago that what Negro leaders there were in a Negro community were what we sometimes call the "accommodating" Negro leaders. They weren't really leaders of organized groups of anything. They were people who were prominent in the community who could guarantee with reasonable certainty that if certain concessions were granted to the Negro community or certain favors, that they could keep the peace. These, I suppose, were Floyd Hunter's runners or a sort of limited runners, but they would communicate to the Negro community. Most of the negotiations of this type between the white power structure and these gatekeepers of the total community were unofficial negotiations.

Well, this type of leadership seems about gone. Research seems to indicate that the Negro community prefers petitions rather than just requests. They prefer to make demands, they prefer to go to court, they prefer the whole notion that what they are seeing is a matter of right rather than a matter of personal favor. And so this seems to be the kind of change that's taking place.

Mr. Myers:

I'd like to make one clarification. I don't want to imply that there is a single stable power structure that lives on and on in each of these communities. In my community we have seen within the past five years the old power structure give way and the new power structure move in with a newspaper as its tool of communication. They were able to elect three members to the city commission, so they are known as the Young Turks and there is a real conflict between two power structures, each vying with the other. I assume that a power structure that wishes to survive in a southern community which faces this problem will have to make a decision as to whether or not it can stand the competition of another power structure.

I'm not suggesting that the school person is going to be leading the other power structure because the evidence indicates he won't, but there must be other people there who are willing to compete, especially in a community that has changed its characteristics and population with new industry in the past ten years. Often times I think we are guilty of feeling that things are going to be awfully tough and we're thinking of things as they used to be and I know that often times we could go much farther than we surmise we can. Do you have any questions to ask our legal man?

Question:

I was at the Gainesville meeting. I have been talking to some of these gentlemen from Georgia and I understand the kinds of information that were passed to us are not necessarily the kind that the group in Georgia got as far as the faculty aspect of these desegregation ideas are concerned. I wonder what the situation really is.

Mr. Knowles:

As I understand, some Assistant Attorney-General decided that he would just tell the boys to file Form 441's and forget this type of stuff. For your information, what Georgia thinks about the faculty desegregation is incorrect and Georgia has changed its mind. But the thing is that when we're talking to you people about the responsibilities, duties and all this, you hate to be had. You hate to start this stuff in good faith and then feel somebody else is going to get a break next door in Georgia, or over in South Carolina. Well, I can assure you officially and unofficially that nobody is getting a break, I can assure you, you are not being had at all and nobody is going to get away with anything less.

Question:

In our group, yesterday, the point came up as to how they are going to enforce this.

Mr. Knowles:

They can enforce it either way. You see, I wasn't there and I can only represent what the thinking was in Washington. If Georgia is saying that they need not consider any faculty desegregation, they're wrong. This is the problem of communication and they just didn't get it but this faculty desegregation is really in the picture and you will start thinking about it today.

In the free choice plans, everybody gets a free choice of schools and we all know that nobody in his right mind did ever give kids a free choice of schools. I mean, how do you run a system? Just draw the lines and make the kids go there? Free choice is a transitional thing. This is what you are doing. You tell everybody that they get a free choice of schools and it lessens the impact on the community. But free choice of schools is a myth. I mean, you wouldn't do this if you had to run a system. Would you give a kid his choice of what school he wants to go to? No. So, you wouldn't do it. But do think about faculty. Anytime you listen to anything you generally hear what you'd like to hear, but in terms of the Georgia impression probably this is what they wanted to hear.

Question:

But if I'm incorrect, I'd like someone to correct me. I thought I was listening to everything at the meeting and faculty was not mentioned.

Question:

But what was wrong with what Georgia heard? I'm from Georgia and I still don't know what was wrong.

Mr. Knowles:

The question is that faculty desegregation was not mentioned in the Georgia explanations, so consequently the assumption is that faculty desegregation does not have to be faced and this is what I am saying is wrong.

Question:

If we signed the letter of compliance, then we did not have to have a plan. Some people think we have to have a plan for desegregation and some say we do not. Now what's the score?

Mr. Knowles:

This is it. When you sign Form 441, you affirm that your system is completely desegregated, that the elements of race do not enter into assignment of any services, including teachers to your children. Now, the next step is the alternative of the plan, and the plan will get accepted quicker than this 441. Off the record, they will hold up the 441 and probably write you a nice letter saying that you must be mistaken. Start thinking about a plan because this is what you have got to do.

Question:

What was the purpose of Form 441?

Mr. Knowles:

The purpose is somewhere in the wisdom of the federal government. I don't know. But I think it is a silly thing. It does lead to misapprehension and this is the trouble. Nobody has been thinking really positively about this. Your State Department is where you have been misled. It's unfortunate, but that's the fact of life.

In your plan, you are going to have either free choice or geographical zoning. If it's going to be free choice, you're going to have to give people a choice. You can't bury the free choice in school board minutes some place where the only person who will read it was the secretary when she typed it. You have to put it in the paper. You are going to have to give the kids the forms. Let them choose their school and inform the parents. Tell them no intimidation.

You're going to have to address yourselves to the problems of school bus desegregation. You have to say that plans are made or give the fundamental part of a desegregating service that the school bus will pick up both colors. You are going to have to address yourself to the problem of faculty desegregation. You're going to have to talk about it in your plan. You don't have to say you're going to do it tomorrow but you're going to have to mention it. Now how long do you have to do it? You have to justify anything less than tomorrow. If you're going to take two years, O. K. perhaps. If you're going to take 20 years, no, or 12 years, no. So, it means that it is going to come in maybe two years.

Dr. Myers:

The kinds of questions that are being asked now are over the heads of the majority of the panel, so we are going to turn it back to Mike and let him set up his own panel.

Mr. Acree:

May I have a word just before we break up because it is so pertinent to these Georgians in particular, and I am from Georgia. I hesitate to do this, but I think it should be done with regard to this question that has been raised with regard to personnel. I have here an answer from the Assistant Attorney General of Georgia to a question posed to him by the chairman of the Board of Education. Would you like to hear it now? I was a bit reluctant to do this but one of the superintendents from Georgia insisted, so I just happened to have this in my possession.

The question posed to the Assistant Attorney General is this and I quote:

Note:

At this point, Mr. Acree read the opinion of the Assistant Attorney General of the State of Georgia.

Dr. Stolee:

We'll start off with some questions that were asked in the small groups and then some will come from the floor. We will ask Mr. Knowles and Mr. Kruger to answer the proper ones. One of the things that has been bothering a couple of superintendents is "What happens if I develop a voluntary plan for desegregation and I send it in to the United States Office of Education and they reject it? What happens then?"

Mr. Kruger:

In response to this specific question, the methods of compliance are Form 441, signed in good faith and assuming requirements are met; a final court order of a United States Court calling for a desegregation plan; or a plan approved by the Commissioner of Education. Now, if the applicant submits a plan and the plan is not approved, and it cannot meet either of these other two alternatives, then the district is not in compliance, and Title VI says federal funds cannot be forthcoming. Specifically that's the answer to that question.

Dr. Stolee:

We understand the date is March 3 when these plans are supposed to be in. The fiscal year for the schools starts July 1. Let's say a plan is submitted, goes through Jim Campbell's office and he sends it on to Washington. What happens? When do we lose our money if the thing is rejected? Do we lose our money or do we get a chance to revise the plan? What sort of thing happens, really, if somebody looks at the plan and he does not like it?

Mr. Kruger:

First of all, I think there has been some confusion about March 3. The more critical date is January 3, because the regulations say that 30 days after publishing the regulations and this was done on December 4, there would be no more new programs approved. Well, we're getting into a rather critical phase here. We've had some instances long before March 3 where we had to hold up the awarding of a grant under Title IV even though the purpose of this grant was to promote some part of the compliances under Title VI. So if a district is receiving direct funds and it makes a new application for funds, March 3 doesn't mean anything. January 3 and thereafter they have to submit compliance forms. I think that the literature that went from our office to the state departments of education requested certain information and the return of materials by March 3. Let's say that a district does not submit Form 441, is not under court order, does not sign a compliance and does not make any application for funds. Title VI isn't really applicable here. You may have some business with the Department of Justice but this may be a different thing entirely. I think that the March 3 deadline is an administrative date that we established with state departments. The real rule is that there will be no new federal monies to anyone after January 3, unless we have some stated compliance. Some districts will continue to receive funds under programs that were approved prior to January 3, but the real date comes when these programs run out and new programs become effective.

THE ST. LOUIS STORY

The Integration of a Public School System

St. Louis Public Schools Instruction Department, February, 1955

Foreword

Since immediatley after the Supreme Court of the United States handed down its historic opinions of May 17, 1954, our office has received inquiries from all sections of the country as to what the Board of Education is planning and doing relative to desegregation of the schools under its control. Most of these inquiries have come from educators in other systems, from professional associations or committees concerned with educational problems, from graduate students of education, and from organizations interested in more or less related social problems.

In order to answer as factually as possible the questions more frequently raised and to share and exchange the essence of our experience in integration with others who, like us, are seeking to comply with the edict of our highest court, we prepared and issued in February, 1955, a resume of how our Board of Education planned to bring about the transition and what had been accomplished towards this end. It is, in broad outline, the St. Louis story of progress in the integration of its public schools. We trust that it will give those inquiring a general concept of what is in process here with respect to implementation of the Supreme Court's decision.

Philip J. Hickey, *Superintendent of Instruction, St. Louis, Missouri*

The St. Louis Story
The Integration of a Public School System

I. *The Supreme Court Renders Its Decision of May 17, 1954.*

On May 17, 1954, the Supreme Court of the United States declared unanimously and unequivocally that racial segregation in public education is in violation of the American Constitution. In the course of the two opinions on this issue handed down on that date, the Justices pointed out that children of a minority group forced to attend segregated public schools were being denied the equal protection of the laws guaranteed by the Fourteenth Amendment and that they were being deprived of liberty without due process of law in violation of the Fifth Amendment.

The opinion in the case of *Brown et al vs. Board of Education of Topeka et al*—which challenged the validity of public school segregation in the states—is based on the findings of modern psychology. To separate Negro children, it points out, "from others of similar age and qualifications solely because of their race generates a feeling of inferiority as to their status in the community that may affect their hearts and minds in a way unlikely ever to be undone." Considerations of this kind, it says, "apply with added force to children in grade and high school."

It further elaborates this point in the following language: "Segregation of white and colored children in public schools has a detrimental effect upon the colored children. The impact is greater when it has the sanction of the law; for the policy of separating the races is usually interpreted as denoting the inferiority of the Negro group. A sense of inferiority affects the motivation of a child to learn. Segregation with the sanction of the law, therefore, has a tendency to retard the educational and mental development of Negro children and to deprive them of some of the benefits they would receive in a racially integrated school system."

"Whatever may have been the extent of psychological knowledge at the time of *Plessy v. Ferguson* (1896) this finding is amply supported by modern authority. Any language in *Plessy v. Ferguson* contrary to this finding is rejected."

In regard to the equality or inequality of tangible factors, the issue is clearly stated and squarely met: "We come then to the question presented: Does segregation of children in public schools solely on the basis of race, even though the physical facilities and other 'tangible factors' may be equal, deprive the children of the minority group of equal educational opportunities? We believe that it does."

And finally, "We conclude that in the field of public education, the doctrine of 'separate but equal' has no place. Separate educational facilities are inherently unequal. Therefore we hold that the plaintiffs and other similarly situated for whom the actions have been brought are, by reason of the segregation complained of, deprived of the equal protection of the laws guaranteed by the Fourteenth Amendment."

The Negro child, the Court held, must be protected from being placed in a situation which creates in him a feeling of inferiority which in turn retards his educational and mental development.

In the case of *Bolling v. Sharpe*—which challenged the validity of public school segregation in the District of Columbia—the Court ruled that denial to a Negro child of the right to attend a public school on the same basis as any other child was to deprive him of liberty without due process of law.

"Liberty under law extends to the full range of conduct which the individual is free to pursue, and it cannot be restricted except for a proper governmental objective. Segregation in public education is not reasonably related to any proper government objective and thus it imposes on Negro children of the District of Columbia a burden that constitutes an arbitrary deprivation of their liberty in violation of the Due Process Clause."

"We hold that racial segregation in the public schools of the District of Columbia is a denial of the due process of law guaranteed by the Fifth Amendment to the Constitution."

Thus the decisions were based on spiritual and mental rather than *physical* grounds. They said that though the tangible features of legally segregated public schools for children of a minority group may be equal or even superior, the fact of segregation *per se* makes them inferior. They affirmed without qualification the constitutional right of all American children to equal protection of the laws and to freedom under the law as far as public school attendance is concerned.

II. *The Board of Education of the City of St. Louis Meets, June 22, 1954. Factors Making for Readiness of St. Louis for the Decision.*

When the decision was announced, the Board of Education of the City of St. Louis and Boards of Education of a number of other localities in Missouri and elsewhere, immediately began to plan to integrate. On June 17, 1954, one month after the date of the decision, a letter was written each member of the Board by its secretary calling a Special Meeting "for the purpose of considering and acting upon the question of desegregation of the schools operated by said Board in the City of St. Louis, as a result of opinion of the Supreme Court of the United States, in the case of *Brown et al vs. Board of Education of Topeka et al.*" This immediate action of the Board symbolized the readiness of the St. Louis community and the St. Louis Public Schools for the change-over.

A number of factors accounted for this readiness. In the first place, the St. Louis community itself had been experiencing a process of democratization over a period of the past ten years. Some examples of this had been (a) condemnation of segregation by the Metropolitan Church Federation and application of the principle of integration in its own organization, (b) emphasis in Catholic churches on the fact that segregation was contrary to Christianity and welcoming of Negro members to unsegregated participation in all phases of church life, (c) desegregation of St. Louis University, (d) desegregation of Catholic elementary and high schools, (e) desegregation of Washington University, (f) increasing desegregation of leading hotels of the city, (g) desegregation of St. Louis' largest legitimate theater, (h) considerable desegregation of housing as a result of the Supreme Court's decision that restrictive covenant classes banning sale of property to Negroes were unenforceable in the courts, and (i) considerable desegregation of employment as illustrated by the hiring of numbers of Negro street car and bus operators.

All changes of this kind had received the strong endorsements of both the Protestant and Catholic Churches and were topics of commendatory editorials on the part of the local press. They had also been specific objectives of a number of social agencies. Thus during the past ten years, the St. Louis community has been in the process of rejecting the principle of segregation and adopting the principle of integration. The Supreme Court's decision was therefore consistent with rather than contrary to the pattern of thought and action which had characterized the progress of the city for the past decade.

A second important factor making for readiness to accept the decision is that there had been over this same period increasing integration of public school teachers and principals of St. Louis in the performance of their professional duties and the operation of their professional organizations. For many years courses of study have been written and textbooks selected for the St. Louis Public Schools by integrated committees of teachers and principals; the city-wide Elementary School Principals Association has always included Negroes in its membership and has during the past few years operated on an integrated basis to a greater extent than previously. As a matter of fact, the present president of this organization happens to be a Negro. Other professional groups, such as the Association for Childhood Education have been more or less completely integrated themselves and active in promoting integration in all professional undertakings.

In 1949, the Missouri State Teachers Association admitted Negro teachers to membership. From that time on, this association, as well as its local subsidiary, has operated on a non-segregated basis. Several years ago, an Intergroup Education Association of teachers and principals—with a present membership of 525 persons—was organized for the purpose of improving the teaching of human relations in the schools. This, of course, was also an integrated group. When the decision came, therefore, the educators of Missouri had already officially rejected the principle of racial segregation in their relationships with one another and were at work implementing the principle of integration in their own ranks.

A third and by no means least important factor which made for readiness to accept and implement the decision on the part of students particularly has been the development over the past ten years of a citywide human relations program conducted on a scientific basis and under expert leadership. Promotion of wholesome human relations has of course always been a primary concern of good teachers everywhere and various methods of accomplishing this objective have been used with educative results throughout the history of the St. Louis Public Schools. The present systematic approach to the problem dates from the winter of 1944-45, when a curriculum committee on Intercultural Relations was appointed to serve in the social studies area of the Courses of Study Council. In May, 1945, the St. Louis Public School System was invited to become a participating system in an eighteen-city experimental study of intergroup education being made by the American Council on Education. The invitation was accepted and active participation began in November, 1945, with the visit to St. Louis of Dr. Hilda Taba, National Director of the Study, Mr. Herbert Walther, Co-ordinator, and Mr. John Robinson, Consultant. From its inception, Mr. Frank Sskwor, now of the faculty of Harris Teachers College, served as local co-ordinator of the project.

This experiment has grown into a systematic human relations program of far-reaching proportions, the purpose of which has been to discover effective means of promoting goodwill and understanding among the various groups of people living in St. Louis. It has concentrated upon the problem of educating boys and girls to live together co-operatively and with mutual understanding and appreciation of each other. This has been attempted partially by direct projects with boys and girls and partially by helping teachers perfect their skills in teaching human relations. From the curricular point of view, the approach has not been the offering of separate courses in human relations but the introduction of materials and techniques in the various areas of learning—art, literature, music, science, etc.—which would conduce to the improvement of human relations. From the extracurricular point of view, some activities found effective have been auditorium programs presented at one high school by pupils of another; formation of an all-city student council meeting monthly to discuss matters of common interest to all teen-agers; an intergroup youth conference sponsored by the National Conference of Christians and Jews in co-operation with public, private, and parochial schools from the city and county, in which one hundred adult leaders from all walks of life have particpated as resource people; interracial letter-writing between schools; and interracial high school athletic events.

Perhaps the most important aspect of the work in this human relations program has been helping teachers acquire skills in assisting pupils to overcome artificial barriers to the acceptance of each individual on his own merits. Well over a hundred St. Louis teachers have attended summer workshops in intergroup education at such places as Washington University, St. Louis University, Harvard, Denver University, Northwestern University, and The University of Chicago, many of them going on scholarships awarded through the National Conference of Christians and Jews. A full-time consultant in human relations has devoted a major portion of his time and energies to helping teachers guide pupils in the art of co-operative living. As has been previously mentioned, an Intergroup Education Association, with a membership of 525 teachers, administrators, and consultants has been formed for the purpose of improving efficiency in this area. This systematic, city-wide program in teaching children the worth and dignity of the individual, which from the point of view of education for good American citizenship it was essential to carry on whether segregation continued or not, has been productive of attitudes and goodwill which greatly facilitated the acceptance and implementation of the Supreme Court's decision. The immediate action of the Board of Education in calling a Special Meeting to consider such implementation, therefore, was symbolic not only of the readiness for integration of the community as a whole and the teaching corps as a whole but of the students as well.

III. *The Board of Education Adopts a Program for Integration of the St. Louis Public Schools.*

At this meeting of June 22, 1954, the board—as elected representatives of the St. Louis community—officially and unanimously adopted a program for integration of the schools under its control by steps, to be begun in September, 1954, and completed by September, 1955. A reason for making the transition by steps over the period of a year was that considerable detail work had to be done in regard to such matters as the drawing of new school district boundaries, assignment of teachers and pupils and other personnel, transfer of books and materials, and transmission of information to parents. To do this work properly required time. Another advantage of integrating the system by steps was that a major portion of administrative attention could then be concentrated on the particular schools being integrated at the time they were being integrated, thus making possible a better supervisory job.

This plan, unanimously approved by the Board, provided (a) for integration of colleges and of special schools and classes in September, 1954; (b) for integration of all high schools under the Board's control, except the technical high schools, and integration of the adult education program at the beginning of the second semester, January 31, 1955; and (c) integration of technical high schools and integration of regular elementary schools in September, 1955.

It stipulated that integrated boundary lines for the general high schools be published by November 15, 1954, and for elementary schools by February 1, 1955. Students, under the plan, are required to attend schools according to these boundaries with the exceptions that (a) the proper school authorities may transfer students from one district to another to relieve overcrowding, and (b) students already enrolled in a school but not resident in its new district may, but are not required to, continue at that school until they graduate, provided the school is not overcrowded.

The plan further stipulated (a) that tenure rights of certificated employees will be preserved, (b) that whenever possible, employees will retain their present assignments, being transferred only to meet the needs of the service, (c) that when vacancies occur employees will be assigned to fill them on the basis of the competence and adaptability of an employee for a particular assignment, (d) that teachers will be appointed from a single rated list on the basis of examination scores, without regard to race or color, (e) that promotions will continue to be made only on the basis of merit, and (f) that vacancies among lunchroom or matron and custodial staff will be filled on the basis of competence and adaptability, that employees in these and other non-certificated classes will be appointed from lists compiled from examination scores, without regard to race or color, and that promotions of such personnel will continue to be made solely on the basis of merit.

The plan thus provided for orderly integration of the schools, minimum interference with the educational programs of students, and maximum protection of the interests of employees and prospective employees.

The Board, in adopting it, made the following statement: "The program we have agreed upon has been prepared without benefit of direction from our state authorities, and it is conceivable that subsequent action by such authorities may dictate some modification of the program. It does, however, represent the best judgment of Board members and school administrators."

On June 30, 1954, Mr. John M. Dalton, Attorney General of the State of Missouri, ruled that provisions of the Missouri Constitution and laws which required the maintenance of separate schools for Negro and white children "are superseded by the decision of the United States Supreme Court and are, therefore, unenforceable." Because of this, he ruled, there are now no valid laws in Missouri which either require or permit segregation of the races in the public schools. This ruling cleared the way for inauguration without modification of the Board's schedule of desegregation.

Both before and after announcement of the plan, many leading organizations of the community volunteered their assistance and support to the Board in carrying out its program. These included the press, the League of Women Voters, the City-

Wide Parent and Patron Organizations and Alliances, the Y.M.C.A., the Y.W.C.A., the N.A.A.C.P., the Urban League, the Metropolitan Church Federation, the Catholic Church, the National Conference of Christians and Jews, the Mayor's Commission on Human Relations, and others. One daily paper endorsed the plan and expressed the hope that the changeover might proceed a little more rapidly than the outlined schedule proposed. The League of Women Voters issued a pamphlet designed to help the public understand and co-operate with what the Board was trying to do. The Metropolitan Church Federation urged all its member churches to devote a portion of their Sunday Services to prayer for the success of public school integration. The Catholic churches of the city urged their parishioners to co-operate fully with the Board of Education in its program of desegregation. The City-Wide Parent and Patron Organizations and Alliances—both white and Negro—pledged their unqualified support, and worked closely with the Superintendent and with each other to make the transition worthy of the best traditions of the city and system. They also made plans for integration on the city-wide parent organization level. The Mayor's Commission on Human Relations conducted a workshop on integration, bringing to the community a number of experts in this area and co-operating closely with the administrative and teaching staff of the public schools. Never has there been a project on which the leadership groups of St. Louis co-operated more unreservedly than they did on this.

IV. *The Board of Education Implements Its Program*

In September, 1954, the first step in implementation of this program was taken. This was integration of the colleges and integration of the special schools and classes. Stowe Teachers College and Stowe Junior College had been an institution with a Negro student body and a Negro teaching and custodial personnel. Harris Teachers College and Harris Junior College had been an institution with a white student body and a white teaching and custodial personnel. The two were combined into one institution and housed in the Harris College Building, with approximately forty per cent of the student body and faculty Negro and sixty per cent of the student body and faculty white. There was also integration of the clerical personnel and custodial staff.

The transition was made without incident and in an atmosphere of friendliness and goodwill—with all concerned determined to see that it was properly consummated. It was, commented one experienced administrator who observed it at first hand, no different from combining two shcools composed of students and teachers of the same race. Much of the credit for the success of this initial step must be attributed to the vigorous democratic leadership which had been developed among the students of both colleges as well as the previoulsy mentioned program of human relations and high degree of integration attained already by the professional staff. It is significant that the enrollment of the integrated college exceeded the sum of the enrollments of the two separate colleges for the previous year. Whatever may have been the causes for this, the fact remains that integration did not result in decreased enrollment. Incidentally, the combination released a building for the housing of five hundred elementary school pupils in an area of the city where pupil-teacher ratio was extremely high.

Integration of special schools and classes was carried out in September, 1954, with equal effectiveness. Turner School for Orthopedically Handicapped Children has been an institution with a Negro student body and was staffed with Negro personnel. Michael School for Orthopedically Handicapped Children had been an institution with a white student body and was staffed with white personnel. The Michael School building was adequate to house the program for all orthopedically handicapped children of the city. The two schools were therefore combined into one and housed in the Michael building. There was complete integration of pupils, teachers, attendants, custodial staff, bus drivers, and therapists. The combination was made without incident and was characterized by a spirit of co-operation on the part of all involved. The two schools for the deaf were similarly integrated. The combination of the schools for the orthopedically handicapped and the combination of the schools for the deaf released desperately needed classroom space for regular elementary school pupils in a densely populated area of the city.

Integration was also quietly but equally successful at the school at Shriners Hospital (where three public school teachers are employed) and at Missouri Hills (formerly Bellefontaine Farms) where socially maladjusted boys are instructed. In the case of classes for mentally retarded pupils, which for the most part are housed in regular elementary school buildings, integrated district lines were drawn and pupils assigned without regard to race. It is worthy of comment that in the five instances in which one Negro pupil attended a special class in a regular elementary school which had not yet been integrated, teachers and principals exercised special care to see that *a happy adjustment* was made.

Desegregation of the general high schools and desegregation of the adult education program were effected as scheduled on January 31, 1955, at the beginning of the second semester. New high school district boundary lines had been drawn on the basis of building capacity, distance, and transportation facilities. They were announced on November 15, 1954. I.B.M. cards used in outlining them contained no data as to race. Students already enrolled in a school but not resident in its new district were granted the option of continuing to attend that school or of transferring to the school in the new district of which they resided.

Results of their selections are indicated by the following report on student population of six of the former white high schools on the opening day of the semester:

Soldan-Blewett	— 350 Negroes out of 1,350 students.
McKinley	— 211 Negroes out of 1,437 students.
Beaumont	— 98 Negroes out of 1,890 students.
Central	— 167 Negroes out of 1,201 students.
Cleveland	— 7 Negroes out of 1,483 students.
Roosevelt	— 29 Negroes out of 1,820 students.

The number of white and Negro students now enrolled in these six schools is not known, as statistics on student population are no longer kept by race.

Largely due to the location of Sumner and Vashon, the two former Negro general high schools, no white pupils were enrolled at these two schools at the beginning of this semester. For the same reason, no Negro pupils were enrolled at Southwest, a former white high school. One educationally helpful result of the integration was that the crowded conditions which had for many years existed at the former Negro high schools were measureably relieved. The principal of one of them was quoted as saying that for the first time since his building was occupied, there was space to turn around. Because of the reduction in enrollment, a number of teachers from the former Negro high schools were transferred to former white high schools where additional teachers were needed because of increased enrollment.

It was the city-wide plan that each high school principal, in cooperation with his faculty and parent, patron, and student groups should assume the responsibility of working out a democratically desirable program for integration of his school. This was done in a variety of ways. Each high school was organized to welcome its new students and to help them orient themselves as speedily and satisfactorily as possible. Each elementary school sending students to high school exercised more than usual care to make the transition successful. High schools transferring pupils to other high schools did likewise. Students took over much of the responsibility for making integration work. This they did through such means as participation in auditorium meetings and writing of articles or editorials for school papers.

As a result, the day of integration was outstandingly successful. It was a "natural school day"—characterized by normalcy. The big news of the day was that there was no "news". It was the quiet and undramatic culmination of years of educational programming and democratic practice and the outcome of contributions to the building of goodwill by many diverse community agencies. It was described in an editorial appearing two days later in the New York Times as an example of what a sound community approach to the problem of desegregation could accomplish.

Integration of the Board's Adult Education Program—including both day and evening classes—proceeded in the same undramatic but significant way that characterized integration of other divisions of the system. The public was informed that the adult education program was to be integrated as of January 31, 1955, and a number of people took advantage of the convenience and increased opportunities afforded.

Two steps of St. Louis' three-step schedule for desegregation have thus been taken. One remains. In September, 1955, the third and final step will be made with integration of the regular elementary schools and integration of the technical high schools.

As stipulated in the Board's plan, integrated elementary school district boundaries which will become effective next September were announced January 30, 1955. These boundaries were drawn taking into account school building capacities, travel distance, and traffic hazards. I.B.M. cards on the basis of which they were outlined contained no data as to racial identity. As in the case of the general high schools, pupils already enrolled in a school but not resident in its new district will be granted the option of continuing to attend that school provided it is not overcrowded or of transferring to the school in the new district in which they reside.

One highly salutary outcome of this elementary school re-districting will be the elimination of the extremely high pupil-teacher ratio which prevails in certain heavily populated areas in the central part of the city. And while the re-districting will not by any means solve the overall problem of pupil-teacher ratio, it will eliminate glaringly incongrous situations in which pupils living within a few blocks of an underpopulated school travel seven or eight miles across the city to a school with a much higher pupil-room ratio or in which a school the pupil population of which exceeds its normal capacity is within a few blocks of a school with vacant rooms. An immediate result will be to make possible, by the erection of primary branch schools in areas of concentrated population, a greatly imporved teacher-pupil ratio and a more equitable distribution of pupils between schools.

Integration of the technical high schools is also scheduled to take place in September, 1955. A new technical high school is now under construction in the southwest part of the city and Hadley—the present technical high school for white students—is being modernized. Upon completion of the new technical high school building, Washington, the present technical high school for Negro students, will be moved to the Hadley building and operated on an integrated basis as a cosmopolitan high school offering technical subjects. This will further ease overpopulation in the high schools in the central part of the city. The new technical high school will also be operated on an integrated basis. The present Washington Technical High School building will be converted to use as an elementary school, which will afford additional opportunity to reduce class size on the elementary level.

V. *Some Anticipated Outcomes of Integration.*

Here, then, we have a bare outline of the St. Louis story of public school integration as it has progressed to this time. It is a story of evolving democracy, of closeknit community co-operation, of professional vision on the part of teachers and principals, of wisdom and intelligent planning on the part of the Board of Education, and of a long-term program of educating boys and girls in wholesome human relations. We believe that it will eventuate in St. Louis' becoming a greater and more democratic American community and in its public school system's becoming a more truly efficient servant of such a community. We believe also that the spiritual and intellectual values the importance of which was so strongly emphasized in the Supreme Court's decision—those great intangibles which make life in our democracy so uniquely worthwhile—will be increasingly realized in our system because of this basic change in its organization. And we are thoroughly convinced that from the economic point of view, the community will receive greater value for its tax dollar because of the elimination of unnecessary duplication of facilities, reduction in expenses of transportation, and elimination of waste in classrooms at a time when classrooms are at a premium. Thus the Board of Education will be enabled to devote a larger proportion of its funds to one of its most urgent problems—reduction of class size.

APPENDIX B

The Cover Letters and Questionnaire

Sheldon Stoff
Stone Hall
Cornell University
Ithaca, New York
Fall, 1963

Dear Sir:

In cooperation with the New York office of the NAACP I am conducting a study which seeks to identify those factors which are significantly involved in the peaceful desegregation of schools. The results of this study may very well prove to be of considerable value in future school racial crises in the North and South.

I am therefore requesting your assistance in obtaining the information asked for in the enclosed questionnaire. Unless you desire to indicate your name and address on the questionnaire (to allow for future communication in the event additional information is sought) you cannot be identified. Therefore, you may be very frank in your answers.

A self-addressed, stamped envelope is enclosed for your convenience.

Sincerely,

Sheldon Stoff

SS:vw

Enclosure

Sheldon Stoff
Stone Hall
Cornell University
Ithaca, New York
Fall, 1963

Dear Sir:

Selected communities in the nation are being sampled in order to obtain a better understanding of the events and background which have been a part of school desegregation. I am requesting your assistance in obtaining the information asked for in the enclosed questionnaire.

Unless you desire to indicate your name on the questionnaire (to allow for future communication in the event additional information is sought) you cannot be identified. Therefore, you may be very frank in your answers. If you wish you may also add comments to any of the questions.

These anonymous questionnaires are a part of research concerning community school desegregation. Your cooperation will insure a greater knowledge of school desegregation than that which presently exists.

A self-addressed, stamped envelope is enclosed for your convenience.

Sincerely,

Sheldon Stoff

SS:vw

Enclosure

Please place a check beside the appropriate answer for each question you answer.

Sample—I will be happy to cooperate with this research project.
1_____Yes 3_____I don't know
2_____No

1. Have *any* (1 or more) Negroes been admitted to the community's public elementary or secondary schools which were formerly white?
1_____Yes 3_____I don't know
2_____No
2. School desegregation took place in our community during the school year
1_____before 1960 4_____1962-63
2_____1960-61 5_____1963-64
3_____1961-62 6_____I don't know
3. Was school desegregation voluntary or ordered by the courts?
1_____Voluntary 3_____I don't know
2_____Ordered by the courts
4. During a period extending 30 days before to 30 days after school (student) desegregation was there *any physical action* taken against any person (Negro or white) which appeared to be connected with school desegregation?
Actions taken may be described as:
1_____Yes 4_____slaps 7_____knifing(s)
2_____No 5_____fist fights 8_____shooting(s)
3_____I don't know 6_____bombing 9_____other
5. During a period extending 30 days before to 30 days after school (student) desegregation was there *any* damage to public or private *property* which appeared to be connected with school desegregation?
Damage may be described as:
1_____Yes 4_____Defacing(s) 7_____Bombing
2_____No 5_____Fire damage 8_____Window breaking
3_____I don't know 6_____Auto damage 9_____Other
6. The number of people in your community is
1_____1-1,499 4_____20,000-49,999
2_____1,500-9,499 5_____50,000 or more
3_____9,500-19,999 6_____I don't know
7. The percentage of Negroes in this community is
1_____0-9% 4_____50-74%
2_____10-24% 5_____75% or more
3_____25-49% 6_____I don't know
8. The total percent of all "minority" (Negro, Indian, Mexican etc.) groups in the community is
1_____0-9% 4_____50-74%
2_____10-24% 5_____75% or more
3_____25-49% 6_____I don't know
9. The percent of your community population which is foreign born (outside of the U.S.A.) is
1_____0-2% 4_____above 10%
2_____3-6% 5_____I don't know
3_____7-10%

To answer the next four questions it will be necessary to understand "median". The median is the point in the *middle* of the distribution.

For example, if a community had 5 families with incomes of

$25,000
$10,000
$5,000
$2,000
$1,000

The median income would be $5,000.

Second example: school years completed

Mr. Smith 11 years
Mr. Hughes 9 years
Mr. Green 8 years
Mr. Jacks 4 years
Mr. Cole 4 years
Mr. Howard 3 years

(Any value between 4-8 years. 6 would be conventionally used.)
The median school years completed would be 6 years.

10. The median income for *all* families in the local population is
 1_____less than $1,499
 2_____$1,500-$2,499
 3_____$2,500-$3,499
 4_____$3,500-$4,499
 5_____$4,500-$5,499
 6_____$5,500-$6,500
 7_____over $6,500
 8_____I don't know
11. The median income for non-white families in the local population is
 1_____less than $1,499
 2_____$1,500-$2,499
 3_____$2,500-$3,499
 4_____$3,500-$4,499
 5_____$4,500-$5,499
 6_____$5,500-$6,500
 7_____over $6,500
 8_____I don't know
12. The median school years completed for the male population of the community (Negro and white) is
 1_____less than 5 years
 2_____5-7 years
 3_____8-10 years
 4_____11-12 years
 5_____over 12 years
 6_____I don't know
13. The median school years completed for the non-white male population of the community is
 1_____less than 5 years
 2_____5-7 years
 3_____8-10 years
 4_____11-12 years
 5_____over 12 years
 6_____I don't know
14. The percent of professional, technical and kindred workers of the total population of the community is
 1_____less than 1%
 2_____1-4%
 3_____5-9%
 4_____10-14%
 5_____15-20%
 6_____over 20%
 7_____I don't know
15. The percent of all dwelling units in the community, sound, with all plumbing facilities is
 1_____less than 35%
 2_____35-44%
 3_____45-64%
 4_____65-74%
 5_____75-84%
 6_____85% and over
 7_____I don't know
16. At the time of school desegregation the *employment levels* (percent employed) of the male, non-white population for your community were, relative to recent past conditions of white employment in your community.
 1_____below average
 2_____average
 3_____above average
 4_____I don't know

17. At the time of school desegregation the *employment levels* (percent employed) of the male, white population for your community were, relative to recent past conditions of white employment in your community
1______below average
2______average
3______above average
4______I don't know

18. During the first school year of desegregation, which percent of the student body of the desegregated school(s) did the Negro students constitute?
1______less than 1%
2______1-9%
3______10-24%
4______25-50%
5______above 50%
6______I don't know

19. Of the total Negro population attending all community public elementary and secondary schools, the percent *attending desegregated* schools during the *first* year was
1______less than 1%
2______1-9%
3______10-24%
4______25-50%
5______above 50%
6______I don't know

20. At the *time* of school desegregation were police on duty in plain clothes?
1______Yes
2______No
3______I don't know

21. Were there Negroes (one or more) on the police force *at the time* of school desegregation?
1______Yes
2______No
3______I don't know

22. Did law enforcement agencies provide positive, immediate, and decisive action designed to support school desegregation?
1______Yes
2______No
3______I don't know

23. Did most labor unions in the community consist of both Negro and white members at the time of school desegregation?
1______Yes
2______No
3______I don't know

24. Prior to school desegregation were there Negro demonstrations seeking broader civil rights?
1______Yes
2______No
3______I don't know

25. Did school desegregation occur before the desegregation of restaurants?
1______Yes
2______No
3______I don't know

26. Did school desegregation occur before the desegregation of community transportation facilities?
1______Yes
2______No
3______I don't know

27. Were the majority of the community's parks, pools, theaters and public sporting arenas desegregated at the time of school desegregation?
1______Yes
2______No
3______I don't know

28. At the time of school desegregation was there a competitive two party political system in the community?
1______Yes
2______No
3______I don't know

29. Prior to and during school desegregation were the newspaper(s), and television generally trying to promote peaceful school desegregation (indicated by favorable articles etc.)?

Newspapers	Television
1_____Yes	5_____Yes
2_____No	6_____No
3_____They didn't commit themselves	7_____They didn't commit themselves
4_____I don't know	8_____I don't know

30. Were some (one or more) local organizations (not predominantly Negro) such as the Rotary, Lions, Urban League etc. working for school desegregation? (Evidenced by speakers, communiques).
1_____Yes 3_____I don't know
2_____No

31. Did the local civic administration (mayor etc.) support (by statements, actions, speeches) school desegregation?
1_____Yes 3_____I don't know
2_____No

32. Was a special effort made to influence community lower class white economic groups in support of school desegregation?
1_____Yes 3_____I don't know
2_____No

33. Was an attempt made to make the white community aware of possible economic advantages of school desegregation?
1_____Yes 3_____I don't know
2_____No

34. Did school desegregation occur before Negroes were freely voting?
1_____Yes 3_____I don't know
2_____No

35. Before school desegregation was there an attempt to alleviate possible fears of venereal disease (syphilis and gonorrhea) problems?
1_____Yes 3_____I don't know
2_____No

36. Were there breaks in residential segregation prior to school desegregation?
1_____Yes 3_____I don't know
2_____No

37. How many respected white community members (non-political) supported initial school desegregation?
1_____0 4_____10 or more
2_____1-3 5_____I don't know
3_____4-9

38. Was school desegregation an
1_____all at once plan (all possible grades and all possible schools) *or*
2_____a gradual plan (few students or 1 grade or 1 school or a limited plan)?
3_____I don't know

39. Were the public schools desegregated before any of the local parochial (church) schools?
1_____Yes 3_____No local parochial schools
2_____No 4_____I don't know

40. Were there, at the time of desegregation of the public schools, any desegregated public schools within
1_____0-14 miles 3_____none within 50 miles
2_____15-50 miles 4_____I don't know

41. Were the school buildings and equipment for the separate Negro and white schools of comparable quality at the time of school desegregation?

1______Yes   3______I don't know
2______No

42. Was the community superintendent or principal of the "white" school a leader in the development of a definite desegregation plan?

1______Yes   3______I don't know
2______No

43. Did the superintendent or principal of the "white" school actively support the desegregation plan? (speeches, articles, etc.)

1______Yes   3______I don't know
2______No

44. Did the superintendent or principal of the "white" school actively support desegregation on *opening day*?

1______Yes   3______I don't know
2______No

45. Did the school board actively support desegregation? (communiques etc.)

1______Yes   3______I don't know
2______No

46. Did school desegregation occur prior to the desegregation of inter-school sports, music programs, student council meetings etc.?

1______Yes   3______I don't know
2______No

47. Was there (to *any* extent) a desegregated faculty prior to or at the same time as school desegregation of students?

1______Prior teacher desegregation
2______Desegregation of teachers with students
3______No teacher desegregation at the time of student desegregation
4______I don't know

48. Did the white school faculty (in general) attempt to prepare the white students for peaceful school desegregation?

1______Yes   3______I don't know
2______No

49. Did school desegregation have the announced support of the local labor unions?

1______Yes   3______I don't know
2______No

50. Was job security promised for *all* (Negroes and white) employed school personnel?

1______Yes   3______I don't know
2______No

51. Was there a special school office or offices for desegregation proceedings?

1______Yes   3______I don't know
2______No

52. Prior to school desegregation was there a course or workshop in intergroup relations for the white faculty?

1______Yes
2______No
3______I don't know

53. Were the teacher's organizations desegregated prior to student desegregation?

1______Yes
2______No
3______I don't know

54. Did any of the local school administration visit or consult with desegregated schools prior to community school desegregation in an attempt to gain useful information?
1_____Yes 3_____I don't know
2_____No
55. Did white educators believe that the academic ability of the average Negro students were equal to that of the average white students prior to school desegregation?
1_____Yes 3_____I don't know
2_____No
56. Was there sufficient classroom space to make an efficient school desegregation possible?
1_____Yes 3_____I don't know
2_____No
57. Were the policies, practices, and actions of the *state educational agencies* favorable to school desegregation?
1_____Yes 3_____I don't know
2_____No
58. At the time of the desegregation of your community's school were two or more nearby (15 miles) school districts cooperating in desegregating their schools at the same time?
1_____Yes 3_____I don't know
2_____No
59. At the time of desegregation were school districts maintained *without regard to race*?
1_____Yes 3_____I don't know
2_____No
60. Was school desegregation for individual Negro pupils permissive or required?
1_____Permissive 3_____I don't know
2_____Required
61. At the time of school desegregation was it indicated that only the top academic Negro students would be involved in initial desegregation?
1_____Yes 3_____I don't know
2_____No
62. Were school transportation facilities desegregated at the same time, or before the school buildings?
1_____before 4_____we have no school transportation facilities
2_____at the same time
3_____they were not desegregated 5_____I don't know
63. At the time of school desegregation did the white school students (school council, officers etc.) issue statements or perform actions in support of the desegregation?
1_____Yes 3_____I don't know
2_____No
64. Prior to school desegregation were Negro students instructed in behavior designed to promote peaceful desegregation?
1_____Yes 3_____I don't know
2_____No
65. Prior to desegregation did some parents of white school children come out in active support of school desegregation?
1_____Yes 3_____I don't know
2_____No

66. Prior to desegregation was the public informed that academic standards would be maintained after school desegregation?
1______Yes 3______I don't know
2______No
67. At the time of school desegregation were there *any* desegregated churches in the community?
1______Yes 3______I don't know
2______No
68. At the time of school desegregation were one or more of the communities "white" churches (or predominately "white") actively supporting school desegregation?
1______Yes, there was support for school desegregation from one or more "white" churches
2______There was *no* support for school desegregation from any "white" church
3______There were *no white* churches in the community
4______There was church support for school desegregation, but it came from outside our community
5______The local "white" churches opposed school desegregation
6______I don't know
69. Prior to school desegregation was there positive cooperation by an intergroup organization such as the NAACP and the school board or the civic administration working for peaceful desegregation? (Evidence counting for positive cooperation would be two or more meetings or a statement indicating a positive working relationship.)
1______There was cooperation between an intergroup organization and the school board
2______There was cooperation between an intergroup organization and the civic administration
3______There was no evidence at any attempt at cooperation
4______Cooperation was attempted but it did not succeed
5______I don't know
70. Prior to school desegregation was there a specific advisory committee formed to help plan *school* desegregation procedures?
1______Yes 3______I don't know
2______No
71. Prior to school desegregation was there a community interracial committee designed to advise on *general* interracial problems?
1______Yes 3______I don't know
2______No
72. Were pamphlets favorable to desegregation distributed to community leaders prior to school desegregation?
1______Yes 3______I don't know
2______No
73. Within the month prior to initial school desegregation was there an *absence* of opposition by individuals (at public school meetings etc.) opposed to school desegregation? (Check all which apply)
1______No local individuals actively opposed our school desegregation
2______Local individuals actively opposed our school desegregation
3______Individuals living outside our community actively opposed our school desegregation
4______The governor of the state actively opposed our school desegregation
5______I don't know

74. Within the month prior to initial school desegregation was there an absence of opposition by *organized* groups (dissemination of organizational literature, etc.) opposed to desegregation? (Check all which apply)

1_____No local organizations opposed our school desegregation
2_____Local organizations opposed our school desegregation
3_____The local civic administration opposed our school desegregation
4_____Organizations from outside our community actively opposed our school desegregation
5_____The state education department actively opposed our school desegregation
6_____I don't know

75. List, in order of importance, the *most important* persons, groups or events which made a significant difference in your community's school desegregation.

1____
2____
3____
4____
5____

76. *Describe,* if you have time, any person, group, or event which *you* feel made a *significant difference* in your community's school desegregation. (If you also have a newspaper or other published report of the situation which you care to forward your help would be *fully appreciated.*) *This description* could help clarify much that happened in your community.

APPENDIX C

SUMMARY TABLE -- MATCHING COMMUNITIES STUDY
Analysis of Variance
Constant I: Favorable Action by the Local Civic Administration

Variables		Sum of Squares	Degrees of Freedom	F
See list in text.	BG-Between Groups WG-Within Groups			*Sig. at .05 **Sig. at .01
1.	BG	0	1.0	0
	WG	0	26.0	0
	Total	0	27.0	0
2.	BG	0	1.0	
	WG	75.7143	26.0	
	Total	75.7143	27.0	0
3.	BG	6.2976	1.0	
	WG	28.6667	26.0	
	Total	34.9643	27.0	5.7118*
4.	BG	13.2435	1.0	
	WG	7.2180	24.0	
	Total	20.4615	25.0	44.0346**
5.	BG	12.3913	1.0	
	WG	7.9549	24.0	
	Total	20.3462	25.0	37.3846**
6.	BG	4.6643	1.0	
	WG	38.4511	24.0	
	Total	43.1154	25.0	2.9113
7.	BG	5.4277	1.0	
	WG	13.5338	24.0	
	Total	18.9615	25.0	9.6251**
8.	BG	4.5600	1.0	
	WG	14.0000	23.0	
	Total	18.5600	24.0	7.4914*
9.	BG	.05573	1.0	
	WG	2.4706	17.0	
	Total	2.5263	18.0	.3835

Variables	Sum of Squares		Degrees of Freedom	F
See list in text.	BG-Between Groups WG-Within Groups			*Sig. at .05 **Sig. at .01
10.	BG	.1548	1.0	
	WG	49.5294	17.0	
	Total	49.6842	18.0	.0531
11.	BG	1.1736	1.0	
	WG	26.4375	16.0	
	Total	27.6111	17.0	.7103
12.	BG	.2000	1.0	
	WG	12.0000	18.0	
	Total	12.2000	19.0	.3000
13.	BG	.8916	1.0	
	WG	11.5294	17.0	
	Total	12.4211	18.0	1.3147
14.	BG	.4034	1.0	
	WG	59.8824	19.0	
	Total	60.2857	20.0	.1280
15.	BG	8.6282	1.0	
	WG	34.5147	19.0	
	Total	43.1429	20.0	4.7497*
16.	BG	2.6957	1.0	
	WG	8.2588	20.0	
	Total	10.9545	21.0	6.5281*
17.	BG	.2801	1.0	
	WG	3.5294	19.0	
	Total	3.8095	20.0	1.5079
18.	BG	1.1478	1.0	
	WG	6.7368	24.0	
	Total	7.8846	25.0	4.0889
19.	BG	5.1154	1.0	
	WG	26.0000	24.0	
	Total	31.1154	25.0	4.7219*
20.	BG	5.5873	1.0	
	WG	16.4511	24.0	
	Total	22.0385	25.0	8.1512**

Variables	Sum of Squares		Degrees of Freedom	F
See list in text.	BG-Between Groups WG-Within Groups			*Sig. at .05 **Sig. at .01
21.	BG	6.5937	1.0	
	WG	18.0602	24.0	
	Total	24.6538	25.0	8.7623**
22.	BG	.2455	1.0	
	WG	17.0588	21.0	
	Total	17.3043	22.0	.3022
23.	BG	.8167	1.0	
	WG	10.1333	18.0	
	Total	10.9500	19.0	1.4507
24.	BG	3.4991	1.0	
	WG	16.9624	24.0	
	Total	20.4615	25.0	4.9509*
25.	BG	.0046	1.0	
	WG	13.5338	24.0	
	Total	13.5385	25.0	.0082
26.	BG	.2976	1.0	
	WG	22.3810	26.0	
	Total	22.6786	27.0	.3457
27.	BG	.1071	1.0	
	WG	4.5714	26.0	
	Total	4.6786	27.0	.6094
28.	BG	.0000	1.0	
	WG	27.4286	26.0	
	Total	27.4286	27.0	.0000
29.	BG	.0214	1.0	
	WG	17.9786	25.0	
	Total	18.0000	26.0	.0298
30.	BG	.1111	1.0	
	WG	6.8333	16.0	
	Total	6.9444	17.0	.2602
31.	BG	.1905	1.0	
	WG	20.6667	26.0	
	Total	20.8571	27.0	.2396

Variables	Sum of Squares		Degrees of Freedom	F
See list in text.	BG-Between Groups WG-Within Groups			*Sig. at .05 **Sig. at .01
32. Constant	-	-	-	
	-	-	-	
	-	-	-	-
33.	BG	.4286	1.0	
	WG	16.5714	26.0	
	Total	17.0000	27.0	.6724
34.	BG	.5833	1.0	
	WG	20.3810	26.0	
	Total	20.9643	27.0	.7442
35.	BG	.1905	1.0	
	WG	18.6667	26.0	
	Total	18.8571	27.0	.2653
36.	BG	.5833	1.0	
	WG	10.0952	26.0	
	Total	10.6786	27.0	1.5024
37.	BG	.0476	1.0	
	WG	14.3810	26.0	
	Total	14.4286	27.0	.0861
38.	BG	.0711	1.0	
	WG	12.3500	17.0	
	Total	12.4211	18.0	.0978
39.	BG	.4286	1.0	
	WG	20.5714	26.0	
	Total	21.0000	27.0	.5417
40.	BG	.6483	1.0	
	WG	21.2647	21.0	
	Total	21.9130	22.0	.6403
41.	BG	1.9566	1.0	
	WG	9.2286	25.0	
	Total	11.1852	26.0	5.3004*
42.	BG	3.0476	1.0	
	WG	24.3810	26.0	
	Total	27.4286	27.0	3.2500

Variables	Sum of Squares		Degrees of Freedom	F
See list in text.	BG-Between Groups WG-Within Groups			*Sig. at .05 **Sig. at .01
43.	BG	1.1905	1.0	
	WG	25.5238	26.0	
	Total	26.7143	27.0	1.2127
44.	BG	.5833	1.0	
	WG	26.0952	26.0	
	Total	26.6786	27.0	.5812
45.	BG	.2976	1.0	
	WG	18.6667	26.0	
	Total	18.9643	27.0	.4145
46.	BG	.1071	1.0	
	WG	25.1429	26.0	
	Total	25.2500	27.0	.1108
47.	BG	2.3333	1.0	
	WG	24.3810	26.0	
	Total	26.7143	27.0	2.4883
48.	BG	.1071	1.0	
	WG	8.0000	26.0	
	Total	8.1071	27.0	.3482
49.	BG	5.2500	1.0	
	WG	13.7143	26.0	
	Total	18.9643	27.0	9.9531**
50.	BG	.4365	1.0	
	WG	7.2157	21.0	
	Total	7.6522	22.0	1.2703
51.	BG	.0476	1.0	
	WG	16.9524	26.0	
	Total	17.0000	27.0	.0730
52.	BG	.0476	1.0	
	WG	20.9524	26.0	
	Total	21.0000	27.0	.0591
53.	BG	.0476	1.0	
	WG	14.9524	26.0	
	Total	15.0000	27.0	.0828

Variables	Sum of Squares		Degrees of Freedom	F
See list in text.	BG-Between Groups WG-Within Groups			*Sig. at .05 **Sig. at .01
54.	BG	.4286	1.0	
	WG	10.2857	26.0	
	Total	10.7143	27.0	1.0833
55.	BG	2.6786	1.0	
	WG	12.2857	26.0	
	Total	14.9643	27.0	5.6686
56.	BG	.2976	1.0	
	WG	12.6667	26.0	
	Total	12.9643	27.0	.6109
57.	BG	.1071	1.0	
	WG	11.1429	26.0	
	Total	11.2500	27.0	.2500
58.	BG	2.3333	1.0	
	WG	23.5238	26.0	
	Total	25.8571	27.0	2.5789
59.	BG	2.6786	1.0	
	WG	18.2857	26.0	
	Total	20.9643	27.0	3.8086
60.	BG	.5833	1.0	
	WG	23.5238	26.0	
	Total	24.1071	27.0	.6447
61.	BG	.2976	1.0	
	WG	26.6667	26.0	
	Total	26.9643	27.0	.2902
62.	BG	.4286	1.0	
	WG	8.2857	26.0	
	Total	8.7143	27.0	1.3448
63.	BG	2.0167	1.0	
	WG	5.7333	18.0	
	Total	7.7500	19.0	6.3314*
64.	BG	.4286	1.0	
	WG	14.5714	26.0	
	Total	15.0000	27.0	.7647

Variables	Sum of Squares		Degrees of Freedom	F
See list in text.	BG-Between Groups WG-Within Groups			*Sig. at .05 **Sig. at .01
65.	BG	.0119	1.0	
	WG	18.6667	26.0	
	Total	18.6786	27.0	.0166
66.	BG	.4286	1.0	
	WG	24.2857	26.0	
	Total	24.7143	27.0	.4588
67.	BG	.5833	1.0	
	WG	22.0952	26.0	
	Total	22.6786	27.0	.6864
68.	BG	.0169	1.0	
	WG	22.0571	25.0	
	Total	22.0741	26.0	.0192
69.	BG	3.3014	1.0	
	WG	60.9386	23.0	
	Total	64.2400	24.0	1.2461
70.	BG	.0857	1.0	
	WG	75.9143	25.0	
	Total	76.0000	26.0	.0282
71.	BG	1.9114	1.0	
	WG	12.6071	25.0	
	Total	14.5185	26.0	3.7903
72.	BG	3.3185	1.0	
	WG	17.2000	25.0	
	Total	20.5185	26.0	4.8234*
73.	BG	.0381	1.0	
	WG	6.6286	25.0	
	Total	6.6667	26.0	.1437
74.	BG	4.1654	1.0	
	WG	16.4500	24.0	
	Total	20.6154	25.0	6.0772*
75.	BG	1.3714	1.0	
	WG	10.6286	25.0	
	Total	12.0000	26.0	3.2258

Variables	Sum of Squares		Degrees of Freedom	F
See list in text.	BG-Between Groups WG-Within Groups			*Sig. at .05 **Sig. at .01
76.	BG	4.2000	1.0	
	WG	7.8000	25.0	
	Total	12.0000	26.0	13.4615**
77.	BG	10.1250	1.0	
	WG	3.5000	22.0	
	Total	13.6250	23.0	63.6429**
78.	BG	.1267	1.0	
	WG	.8333	23.0	
	Total	.9600	24.0	3.4960
79.	BG	4.0951	1.0	
	WG	9.7895	24.0	
	Total	13.8846	25.0	10.0397**
80.	BG	.7314	1.0	
	WG	23.4286	23.0	
	Total	24.1600	24.0	.0718

Constant II: Community Size

Variables	Sum of Squares		Degrees of Freedom	F
1.	BG	.0000	1.0	
	WG	.0000	26.0	
	Total	.0000	27.0	.0000
2.	BG	2.6786	1.0	
	WG	80.5714	26.0	
	Total	83.2500	27.0	.8644
3.	BG	3.4405	1.0	
	WG	60.6667	26.0	
	Total	64.1071	27.0	1.4745
4.	BG	12.9537	1.0	
	WG	7.2064	23.0	
	Total	20.1600	24.0	41.3433**
5.	BG	12.9537	1.0	
	WG	7.2064	23.0	
	Total	20.1600	24.0	41.3433**

Variables See list in text.	Sum of Squares BG-Between Groups WG-Within Groups		Degrees of Freedom	F *Sig. at .05 **Sig. at .01
6. Constant	-	-	-	
	-	-	-	
	-	-	-	-
7.	BG	.5337	1.0	
	WG	9.7064	23.0	
	Total	10.2400	24.0	1.2645
8.	BG	1.3889	1.0	
	WG	8.4444	22.0	
	Total	9.8333	23.0	3.6184
9.	BG	.0357	1.0	
	WG	1.7143	14.0	
	Total	1.7500	15.0	.2916
10.	BG	2.4000	1.0	
	WG	11.6000	10.0	
	Total	14.0000	11.0	2.0690
11.	BG	.9000	1.0	
	WG	7.5000	8.0	
	Total	8.4000	9.0	.9600
12.	BG	.5051	1.0	
	WG	6.2222	9.0	
	Total	6.7273	10.0	.7305
13.	BG	.8167	1.0	
	WG	6.1000	10.0	
	Total	6.9167	11.0	1.3388
14.	BG	.3750	1.0	
	WG	31.8750	10.0	
	Total	32.2500	11.0	.1176
15.	BG	.1786	1.0	
	WG	29.2500	12.0	
	Total	29.4286	13.0	.0732
16.	BG	1.6770	1.0	
	WG	8.1412	20.0	
	Total	9.8182	21.0	4.1198

Variables	Sum of Squares		Degrees of Freedom	F
See list in text.	BG-Between Groups WG-Within Groups			*Sig. at .05 **Sig. at .01
17.	BG	.3509	1.0	
	WG	3.3333	17.0	
	Total	3.6842	18.0	1.7895
18.	BG	.0212	1.0	
	WG	.9333	20.0	
	Total	.9545	21.0	.4545
19.	BG	.0761	1.0	
	WG	1.7500	21.0	
	Total	1.8261	22.0	.9130
20.	BG	2.3618	1.0	
	WG	19.4643	21.0	
	Total	21.8261	22.0	2.5482
21.	BG	1.6910	1.0	
	WG	19.1786	21.0	
	Total	20.8696	22.0	1.8516
22.	BG	3.2191		
	WG	9.7333	19.0	
	Total	12.9524	20.0	6.2838*
23.	BG	.8167	1.0	
	WG	10.1333	18.0	
	Total	10.9500	19.0	1.4507
24.	BG	1.3059	1.0	
	WG	20.6071	21.0	
	Total	21.9130	22.0	1.3308
25.	BG	.2314	1.0	
	WG	19.9286	23.0	
	Total	20.1600	24.0	.2671
26.	BG	.0003	1.0	
	WG	23.0397	23.0	
	Total	23.0400	24.0	.0003
27.	BG	2.2400	1.0	
	WG	16.0000	23.0	
	Total	18.2400	24.0	3.2200

Variables	Sum of Squares		Degrees of Freedom	F
See list in text.	BG-Between Groups WG-Within Groups			*Sig. at .05 **Sig. at .01
28.	BG	.1829	1.0	
	WG	22.8571	23.0	
	Total	23.0400	24.0	.1840
29.	BG	.6926	1.0	
	WG	14.7619	20.0	
	Total	15.4545	21.0	.9384
30.	BG	.0169	1.0	
	WG	11.1410	17.0	
	Total	11.1579	18.0	.0257
31.	BG	.0003	1.0	
	WG	19.0397	23.0	
	Total	19.0400	24.0	.0004
32.	BG	.0003	1.0	
	WG	21.0397	23.0	
	Total	21.0400	24.0	.0003
33.	BG	1.2203	1.0	
	WG	16.5397	23.0	
	Total	17.7600	24.0	1.6970
34.	BG	1.2203	1.0	
	WG	18.5397	23.0	
	Total	19.7600	24.0	1.5139
35.	BG	.0203	1.0	
	WG	10.5397	23.0	
	Total	10.5600	24.0	.0443
36.	BG	.1829	1.0	
	WG	8.8571	23.0	
	Total	9.0400	24.0	.4748
37.	BG	1.6457	1.0	
	WG	19.7143	23.0	
	Total	21.3600	24.0	1.9200
38.	BG	2.4989	1.0	
	WG	24.4423	15.0	
	Total	26.9412	16.0	1.5335

Variables	Sum of Squares		Degrees of Freedom	F
See list in text.	BG-Between Groups WG-Within Groups			*Sig. at .05 **Sig. at .01
39.	BG	.1269	1.0	
	WG	15.8730	23.0	
	Total	16.0000	24.0	.1840
40.	BG	.1880	1.0	
	WG	17.0294	21.0	
	Total	17.2174	22.0	.2318
41.	BG	1.5114	1.0	
	WG	15.9286	23.0	
	Total	17.4400	24.0	2.1824
42.	BG	8.7479	1.0	
	WG	9.4920	23.0	
	Total	18.2400	24.0	21.1969**
43.	BG	.2017	1.0	
	WG	21.7983	22.0	
	Total	22.0000	23.0	.2035
44.	BG	.0476	1.0	
	WG	27.8095	26.0	
	Total	27.8571	27.0	.0445
45.	BG	.7619	1.0	
	WG	16.0952	26.0	
	Total	16.8571	27.0	1.2308
46.	BG	.4892	1.0	
	WG	21.8071	25.0	
	Total	22.2963	26.0	.5608
47.	BG	1.4405	1.0	
	WG	22.6667	26.0	
	Total	24.1071	27.0	1.6523
48.	BG	.0066	1.0	
	WG	9.1786	25.0	
	Total	9.1852	26.0	.0180
49.	BG	2.6786	1.0	
	WG	20.5714	26.0	
	Total	23.2500	27.0	3.3854

Variables	Sum of Squares		Degrees of Freedom	F
See list in text.	BG-Between Groups WG-Within Groups			*Sig. at .05 **Sig. at .01
50.	BG	.5185	1.0	
	WG	12.0000	25.0	
	Total	12.5185	26.0	1.0803
51.	BG	.0000	1.0	
	WG	16.8571	26.0	
	Total	16.8571	27.0	.0000
52.	BG	.0476	1.0	
	WG	24.3810	26.0	
	Total	24.4286	27.0	.0508
53.	BG	.0119	1.0	
	WG	14.6667	26.0	
	Total	14.6786	27.0	.0211
54.	BG	1.7143	1.0	
	WG	15.1429	26.0	
	Total	16.8571	27.0	2.9434
55.	BG	1.9022	1.0	
	WG	11.7500	21.0	
	Total	13.6522	22.0	3.3996
56.	BG	3.8913	1.0	
	WG	99.9549	24.0	
	Total	103.846	25.0	.9343
57.	BG	.2603	1.0	
	WG	11.2782	24.0	
	Total	11.5385	25.0	.5538
58.	BG	5.4098	1.0	
	WG	66.6643	25.0	
	Total	72.0741	26.0	2.0287
59.	BG	3.1883	1.0	
	WG	17.1579	24.0	
	Total	20.3462	25.0	4.4597*
60.	BG	.3813	1.0	
	WG	27.2437	22.0	
	Total	27.6250	23.0	.3079

Variables	Sum of Squares		Degrees of Freedom	F
See list in text.	BG-Between Groups WG-Within Groups			*Sig. at .05 **Sig. at .01
61.	BG	.0126	1.0	
	WG	20.4874	22.0	
	Total	20.5000	23.0	.0135
62.	BG	.1157	1.0	
	WG	26.3459	24.0	
	Total	26.4615	25.0	.1054
63.	BG	1.8570	1.0	
	WG	16.5778	21.0	
	Total	18.4348	22.0	2.3524
64.	BG	1.8337	1.0	
	WG	15.2063	23.0	
	Total	17.0400	24.0	2.7734
65.	BG	.1679	1.0	
	WG	11.9921	23.0	
	Total	12.1600	24.0	.3221
66.	BG	.9257	1.0	
	WG	17.7143	23.0	
	Total	18.6400	24.0	1.2019
67.	BG	.0384	1.0	
	WG	21.8106	23.0	
	Total	21.8400	24.0	.0405
68.	BG	.0917	1.0	
	WG	22.4683	23.0	
	Total	22.5600	24.0	.0939
69.	BG	1.0019	1.0	
	WG	50.2708	20.0	
	Total	51.2727	21.0	.3986
70.	BG	1.7857	1.0	
	WG	52.2143	23.0	
	Total	54.0000	24.0	.7866
71.	BG	.3429	1.0	
	WG	21.6571	25.0	
	Total	22.0000	26.0	.3958

Variables	Sum of Squares		Degrees of Freedom	F
See list in text.	BG-Between Groups WG-Within Groups			*Sig. at .05 **Sig. at .01
72.	BG	.3241	1.0	
	WG	25.7500	25.0	
	Total	26.0741	26.0	.3146
73.	BG	.5122	1.0	
	WG	16.2286	25.0	
	Total	16.7407	26.0	.7890
74.	BG	1.3962	1.0	
	WG	20.4500	24.0	
	Total	21.8462	25.0	1.6385
75.	BG	1.1177	1.0	
	WG	11.1786	25.0	
	Total	12.2963	26.0	2.4997
76.	BG	1.2963	1.0	
	WG	19.0000	25.0	
	Total	20.2963	26.0	1.7056
77.	BG	3.3346	1.0	
	WG	18.0500	24.0	
	Total	21.3846	25.0	4.4338*
78.	BG	.0051	1.0	
	WG	6.0333	24.0	
	Total	6.0385	25.0	.0204
79.	BG	1.5685	1.0	
	WG	18.9500	25.0	
	Total	20.5185	26.0	2.0693
80.	BG	1.6511	1.0	
	WG	9.9786	25.0	
	Total	11.6296	26.0	4.1365

Constant III: Per Cent of Negroes in the Population

Variables	Sum of Squares		Degrees of Freedom	F
1.	BG	.0476	1.0	
	WG	3.8095	26.0	
	Total	3.8571	27.0	.3250

Variables	Sum of Squares		Degrees of Freedom	F
See list in text.	BG-Between Groups WG-Within Groups			*Sig. at .05 **Sig. at .01
2.	BG	.0476	1.0	
	WG	70.3810	26.0	
	Total	70.4286	27.0	.0176
3.	BG	2.6786	1.0	
	WG	46.5714	26.0	
	Total	49.2500	27.0	1.4954
4.	BG	13.7619	1.0	
	WG	7.2381	26.0	
	Total	21.0000	27.0	49.4342**
5.	BG	13.7619	1.0	
	WG	7.2381	26.0	
	Total	21.0000	27.0	49.4342**
6.	BG	8.6786	1.0	
	WG	46.2587	26.0	
	Total	54.9643	27.0	4.8750*
7. Constant	-	-	-	
	-	-	-	
	-	-	-	-
8.	BG	.0462	1.0	
	WG	7.8000	24.0	
	Total	7.8462	25.0	.1420
9.	BG	.0062	1.0	
	WG	.9412	17.0	
	Total	.9474	18.0	.1118
10.	BG	.0000	1.0	
	WG	20.0000	16.0	
	Total	20.0000	17.0	.0000
11.	BG	.2232	1.0	
	WG	5.2143	14.0	
	Total	5.4375	15.0	.5993
12.	BG	.0625	1.0	
	WG	4.4375	16.0	
	Total	4.5000	17.0	.2254

Variables	Sum of Squares		Degrees of Freedom	F
See list in text.	BG-Between Groups WG-Within Groups			*Sig. at .05 **Sig. at .01
13.	BG	.1111	1.0	
	WG	7.0000	16.0	
	Total	7.1111	17.0	.2539
14.	BG	.7500	1.0	
	WG	39.0000	14.0	
	Total	39.7500	15.0	.2692
15.	BG	.0916	1.0	
	WG	37.6731	15.0	
	Total	37.7647	16.0	.0365
16.	BG	.9689	1.0	
	WG	8.9895	22.0	
	Total	9.9583	23.0	2.3711
17.	BG	.1465	1.0	
	WG	5.1579	21.0	
	Total	5.3044	22.0	.5963
18.	BG	.5833	1.0	
	WG	4.6667	26.0	
	Total	5.2500	27.0	3.2500
19.	BG	1.4405	1.0	
	WG	19.2381	26.0	
	Total	20.6787	27.0	1.9468
20.	BG	5.7619	1.0	
	WG	16.9524	26.0	
	Total	22.7143	27.0	8.8371**
21.	BG	3.4405	1.0	
	WG	23.2381	26.0	
	Total	26.6786	27.0	3.8494
22.	BG	.9346	1.0	
	WG	18.9500	24.0	
	Total	19.8846	25.0	1.1837
23.	BG	3.2535	1.0	
	WG	14.5647	20.0	
	Total	17.8182	21.0	4.4676*

Variables	Sum of Squares		Degrees of Freedom	F
See list in text.	BG-Between Groups WG-Within Groups			*Sig. at .05 **Sig. at .01
24.	BG	1.7143	1.0	
	WG	24.0000	26.0	
	Total	25.7143	27.0	1.8571
25.	BG	.1071	1.0	
	WG	20.5714	26.0	
	Total	20.6786	27.0	.1354
26.	BG	.3975	1.0	
	WG	21.4286	21.0	
	Total	21.8261	22.0	.3896
27.	BG	2.0119	1.0	
	WG	16.9524	26.0	
	Total	18.9643	27.0	3.0857
28.	BG	.0476	1.0	
	WG	27.8095	26.0	
	Total	27.8571	27.0	.0445
29.	BG	.0011	1.0	
	WG	19.6286	25.0	
	Total	19.6296	26.0	.0013
30.	BG	.2667	1.0	
	WG	9.7333	14.0	
	Total	10.0000	15.0	.3836
31.	BG	.0476	1.0	
	WG	20.3810	26.0	
	Total	20.4286	27.0	.0607
32.	BG	.1905	1.0	
	WG	20.6667	26.0	
	Total	20.8571	27.0	.2396
33.	BG	.7619	1.0	
	WG	18.0952	26.0	
	Total	18.8571	27.0	1.0947
34.	BG	1.4405	1.0	
	WG	20.6667	26.0	
	Total	22.1071	27.0	1.8122

Variables	Sum of Squares		Degrees of Freedom	F
See list in text.	BG-Between Groups WG-Within Groups			*Sig. at .05 **Sig. at .01
35.	BG	.0476	1.0	
	WG	10.6667	26.0	
	Total	10.7143	27.0	.1161
36.	BG	1.4405	1.0	
	WG	15.5238	26.0	
	Total	16.9643	27.0	2.4126
37.	BG	1.7143	1.0	
	WG	23.7143	26.0	
	Total	25.4286	27.0	1.8795
38.	BG	.0554	1.0	
	WG	11.8269	15.0	
	Total	11.8824	16.0	.0703
39.	BG	1.1905	1.0	
	WG	23.2381	26.0	
	Total	24.4286	27.0	1.3320
40.	BG	.0048	1.0	
	WG	15.2333	19.0	
	Total	15.2381	20.0	.0059
41.	BG	.7619	1.0	
	WG	12.0952	26.0	
	Total	12.8571	27.0	1.6378
42.	BG	3.8571	1.0	
	WG	22.8571	26.0	
	Total	26.7143	27.0	4.3875*
43.	BG	1.4405	1.0	
	WG	23.8095	26.0	
	Total	25.2500	27.0	1.5730
44.	BG	1.7143	1.0	
	WG	24.0000	26.0	
	Total	25.7143	27.0	1.8571
45.	BG	.5833	1.0	
	WG	14.3810	26.0	
	Total	14.9643	27.0	1.0546

Variables	Sum of Squares		Degrees of Freedom	F
See list in text.	BG-Between Groups WG-Within Groups			*Sig. at .05 **Sig. at .01
46.	BG	.1905	1.0	
	WG	23.5238	26.0	
	Total	23.7143	27.0	.2105
47.	BG	3.4405	1.0	
	WG	23.2381	26.0	
	Total	26.6786	27.0	3.8494
48.	BG	.4286	1.0	
	WG	3.4286	26.0	
	Total	3.8571	27.0	3.2500
49.	BG	4.7619	1.0	
	WG	14.0952	26.0	
	Total	18.8571	27.0	8.7838**
50.	BG	.4365	1.0	
	WG	7.2157	21.0	
	Total	7.6522	22.0	1.2703
51.	BG	.5833	1.0	
	WG	21.5238	26.0	
	Total	22.1071	27.0	.7046
52.	BG	.0000	1.0	
	WG	20.8571	26.0	
	Total	20.8571	27.0	.0000
53.	BG	.4286	1.0	
	WG	20.0000	26.0	
	Total	20.4286	27.0	.5571
54.	BG	.9643	1.0	
	WG	13.1429	26.0	
	Total	14.1071	27.0	1.9076
55.	BG	.1071	1.0	
	WG	18.5714	26.0	
	Total	18.6786	27.0	.1500
56.	BG	.1071	1.0	
	WG	12.5714	26.0	
	Total	12.6786	27.0	.2216

Variables	Sum of Squares		Degrees of Freedom	F
See list in text.	BG-Between Groups WG-Within Groups			*Sig. at .05 **Sig. at .01
57.	BG	1.1905	1.0	
	WG	17.8095	26.0	
	Total	19.0000	27.0	1.7380
58.	BG	4.7619	1.0	
	WG	16.6667	26.0	
	Total	21.4286	27.0	7.4286*
59.	BG	.7619	1.0	
	WG	10.9524	26.0	
	Total	11.7143	27.0	1.8087
60.	BG	.0119	1.0	
	WG	18.9524	26.0	
	Total	18.9643	27.0	.0163
61.	BG	.1905	1.0	
	WG	20.6667	26.0	
	Total	20.8571	27.0	.2396
62.	BG	.0000	1.0	
	WG	16.8571	26.0	
	Total	16.8571	27.0	.0000
63.	BG	.3316	1.0	
	WG	6.3000	17.0	
	Total	6.6316	18.0	.8947
64.	BG	1.7143	1.0	
	WG	18.0000	26.0	
	Total	19.7143	27.0	2.4762
65.	BG	.0000	1.0	
	WG	18.8571	26.0	
	Total	18.8571	27.0	.0000
66.	BG	.9643	1.0	
	WG	19.7143	26.0	
	Total	20.6786	27.0	1.2717
67.	BG	.1905	1.0	
	WG	21.8095	26.0	
	Total	22.0000	27.0	.2271

Variables	Sum of Squares		Degrees of Freedom	F
See list in text.	BG-Between Groups WG-Within Groups			*Sig. at .05 **Sig. at .01
68.	BG	.0000	1.0	
	WG	25.4286	26.0	
	Total	25.4286	27.0	.0000
69.	BG	1.3889	1.0	
	WG	59.1111	22.0	
	Total	60.5000	23.0	.5169
70.	BG	.9643	1.0	
	WG	91.7143	26.0	
	Total	92.6786	27.0	.2734
71.	BG	.0476	1.0	
	WG	23.8095	26.0	
	Total	23.8571	27.0	.0520
72.	BG	.2976	1.0	
	WG	27.8095	26.0	
	Total	28.1071	27.0	.2783
73.	BG	.0119	1.0	
	WG	10.0952	26.0	
	Total	10.1071	27.0	.0307
74.	BG	3.0347	1.0	
	WG	17.6053	23.0	
	Total	20.6400	24.0	3.9647
75.	BG	.7619	1.0	
	WG	16.0952	26.0	
	Total	16.8571	27.0	1.2308
76.	BG	3.8571	1.0	
	WG	10.5714	26.0	
	Total	14.4286	27.0	9.4865**
77.	BG	5.0885	1.0	
	WG	12.4500	24.0	
	Total	17.5385	25.0	9.8091**
78.	BG	.0051	1.0	
	WG	4.0333	24.0	
	Total	4.0385	25.0	.0305

Variables	Sum of Squares		Degrees of Freedom	F
See list in text.	BG-Between Groups WG-Within Groups			*Sig. at .05 **Sig. at .01
79.	BG	1.2963	1.0	
	WG	17.0000	25.0	
	Total	18.2963	26.0	1.9063
80.	BG	.8899	1.0	
	WG	11.6286	25.0	
	Total	12.5185	26.0	1.9132

Constant IV: Income

Variables	Sum of Squares		Degrees of Freedom	F
1.	BG	.1071	1.0	
	WG	8.5714	26.0	
	Total	8.6786	27.0	.3250
2.	BG	5.7619	1.0	
	WG	36.0952	26.0	
	Total	41.8571	27.0	4.1504
3.	BG	3.4405	1.0	
	WG	26.6667	26.0	
	Total	32.1071	27.0	3.1204
4.	BG	15.4286	1.0	
	WG	3.4286	26.0	
	Total	18.8571	26.0	117.0000**
5.	BG	15.4286	1.0	
	WG	3.4286	26.0	
	Total	18.8571	27.0	117.0000**
6.	BG	9.8542	1.0	
	WG	38.6643	25.0	
	Total	48.5185	26.0	6.3717*
7.	BG	2.6099	1.0	
	WG	17.4286	24.0	
	Total	20.0385	25.0	3.5940
8.	BG	1.6806	1.0	
	WG	18.2778	22.0	
	Total	19.9583	23.0	2.0228

Variables	Sum of Squares		Degrees of Freedom	F
See list in text.	BG-Between Groups WG-Within Groups			*Sig. at .05 **Sig. at .01
9.	BG	.0357	1.0	
	WG	1.7143	14.0	
	Total	1.7500	15.0	.2917
10. Constant	-	-	-	
	-	-	-	
	-	-	-	-
11.	BG	.5079	1.0	
	WG	9.7143	7.0	
	Total	10.2222	8.0	.3660
12.	BG	.0000	1.0	
	WG	6.0000	10.0	
	Total	6.0000	11.0	.0000
13.	BG	.5051	1.0	
	WG	4.2222	9.0	
	Total	4.7273	10.0	1.0766
14.	BG	2.3143	1.0	
	WG	36.9000	12.0	
	Total	39.2143	13.0	.7526
15.	BG	3.4220	1.0	
	WG	43.5192	15.0	
	Total	46.9412	16.0	1.1795
16.	BG	.8167	1.0	
	WG	4.9333	18.0	
	Total	5.7500	19.0	2.9797
17.	BG	.1263	1.0	
	WG	2.4000	17.0	
	Total	2.5263	18.0	.8947
18.	BG	1.7146	1.0	
	WG	12.6316	24.0	
	Total	14.3462	25.0	3.2577
19.	BG	1.2963	1.0	
	WG	13.0000	25.0	
	Total	14.2963	26.0	2.4929

Variables	Sum of Squares		Degrees of Freedom	F
See list in text.	BG-Between Groups WG-Within Groups			*Sig. at .05 **Sig. at .01
20.	BG	7.7357	1.0	
	WG	14.2643	25.0	
	Total	22.0000	26.0	13.5578**
21.	BG	8.1270	1.0	
	WG	15.8730	23.0	
	Total	24.0000	24.0	11.7760**
22.	BG	.3836	1.0	
	WG	21.5294	21.0	
	Total	21.9130	22.0	.3742
23.	BG	1.3754	1.0	
	WG	7.9579	22.0	
	Total	9.3333	23.0	3.8024
24.	BG	3.0476	1.0	
	WG	19.8095	26.0	
	Total	22.8571	27.0	4.0000
25.	BG	.0119	1.0	
	WG	14.0952	26.0	
	Total	14.1071	27.0	.0220
26.	BG	.0046	1.0	
	WG	21.5338	24.0	
	Total	21.5385	25.0	.0052
27.	BG	.6352	1.0	
	WG	10.5500	25.0	
	Total	11.1852	26.0	1.5052
28.	BG	.3429	1.0	
	WG	23.6571	25.0	
	Total	24.0000	26.0	.3623
29.	BG	.6119	1.0	
	WG	9.8496	24.0	
	Total	10.4615	25.0	1.4910
30.	BG	.1894	1.0	
	WG	8.5833	20.0	
	Total	8.7727	21.0	.4413

Variables	Sum of Squares		Degrees of Freedom	F
See list in text.	BG-Between Groups WG-Within Groups			*Sig. at .05 **Sig. at .01
31.	BG	.1905	1.0	
	WG	18.6667	26.0	
	Total	18.8571	27.0	.2653
32.	BG	.0677	1.0	
	WG	20.2286	25.0	
	Total	20.2963	26.0	.0837
33.	BG	.2976	1.0	
	WG	16.6667	26.0	
	Total	16.9643	27.0	.4643
34.	BG	.7619	1.0	
	WG	22.0952	26.0	
	Total	22.8571	27.0	.8965
35.	BG	.0476	1.0	
	WG	10.6667	26.0	
	Total	10.7143	27.0	.1161
36.	BG	.0476	1.0	
	WG	8.6667	26.0	
	Total	8.7143	27.0	.1429
37.	BG	.1071	1.0	
	WG	20.8571	26.0	
	Total	20.9643	27.0	.1336
38.	BG	2.8929	1.0	
	WG	21.1071	16.0	
	Total	24.0000	17.0	2.1929
39.	BG	2.0119	1.0	
	WG	23.2381	26.0	
	Total	25.2500	27.0	2.2510
40.	BG	.0555	1.0	
	WG	17.7778	22.0	
	Total	17.8333	23.0	
41.	BG	2.2394	1.0	
	WG	12.3759	24.0	
	Total	14.6154	25.0	4.3428*

Variables	Sum of Squares		Degrees of Freedom	F
See list in text.	BG-Between Groups WG-Within Groups			*Sig. at .05 **Sig. at .01
42.	BG	2.7524	1.0	
	WG	23.9143	25.0	
	Total	26.6667	26.0	2.8773
43.	BG	.4286	1.0	
	WG	27.4286	26.0	
	Total	27.8571	27.0	.4063
44.	BG	.2976	1.0	
	WG	26.6667	26.0	
	Total	26.9643	27.0	.2902
45.	BG	.2122	1.0	
	WG	16.2286	25.0	
	Total	16.7407	26.0	.7890
46.	BG	.4286	1.0	
	WG	24.0000	26.0	
	Total	24.4286	27.0	.4643
47.	BG	.7619	1.0	
	WG	20.0952	26.0	
	Total	20.8571	27.0	.9858
48.	BG	.2881	1.0	
	WG	4.3786	25.0	
	Total	4.6667	26.0	1.6449
49.	BG	3.8571	1.0	
	WG	18.5714	26.0	
	Total	22.4286	27.0	5.4000*
50.	BG	.1705	1.0	
	WG	5.5686	21.0	
	Total	5.7391	22.0	.6430
51.	BG	.0003	1.0	
	WG	16.3459	24.0	
	Total	16.3462	25.0	.0004
52.	BG	.7619	1.0	
	WG	12.9524	26.0	
	Total	13.7143	27.0	1.5294

Variables	Sum of Squares		Degrees of Freedom	F
See list in text.	BG-Between Groups WG-Within Groups			*Sig. at .05 **Sig. at .01
53.	BG	.0476	1.0	
	WG	16.9524	26.0	
	Total	17.0000	27.0	.0730
54.	BG	.7619	1.0	
	WG	12.9524	26.0	
	Total	13.7143	27.0	1.5294
55.	BG	.5833	1.0	
	WG	22.6667	26.0	
	Total	23.2500	27.0	.6691
56.	BG	.1905	1.0	
	WG	14.6667	26.0	
	Total	14.8571	27.0	.3377
57.	BG	.1071	1.0	
	WG	.8571	26.0	
	Total	.9643	27.0	3.2500
58.	BG	8.3820	1.0	
	WG	11.9143	25.0	
	Total	20.2963	26.0	17.5882**
59.	BG	3.3185	1.0	
	WG	17.2000	25.0	
	Total	20.5185	26.0	4.8234*
60.	BG	.9209	1.0	
	WG	22.2643	25.0	
	Total	23.1852	26.0	1.0341
61.	BG	.0119	1.0	
	WG	25.2381	26.0	
	Total	25.2500	27.0	.0123
62.	BG	.1071	1.0	
	WG	14.0000	26.0	
	Total	14.1071	27.0	.1990
63.	BG	2.8339	1.0	
	WG	11.7375	19.0	
	Total	14.5714	20.0	4.5874*

Variables	Sum of Squares		Degrees of Freedom	F
See list in text.	BG-Between Groups WG-Within Groups			*Sig. at .05 **Sig. at .01
64.	BG	.0476	1.0	
	WG	6.6667	26.0	
	Total	6.7143	27.0	.1857
65.	BG	.5598	1.0	
	WG	17.5143	25.0	
	Total	18.0741	26.0	.7990
66.	BG	.1905	1.0	
	WG	21.5238	26.0	
	Total	21.7143	27.0	.2300
67.	BG	.1905	1.0	
	WG	23.8095	26.0	
	Total	24.0000	27.0	.2080
68.	BG	.7619	1.0	
	WG	20.0952	26.0	
	Total	20.8571	27.0	.9858
69.	BG	3.8470	1.0	
	WG	51.8922	21.0	
	Total	55.7391	22.0	1.5568
70.	BG	1.4405	1.0	
	WG	52.6667	26.0	
	Total	54.1071	27.0	.7111
71.	BG	.7619	1.0	
	WG	20.0952	26.0	
	Total	20.8571	27.0	.9857
72.	BG	2.6786	1.0	
	WG	20.2857	26.0	
	Total	22.9643	27.0	3.4331
73.	BG	.4286	1.0	
	WG	1.4286	26.0	
	Total	1.8571	27.0	2.8000**
74.	BG	5.0885	1.0	
	WG	16.4500	24.0	
	Total	21.5385	25.0	7.4239*

Variables	Sum of Squares		Degrees of Freedom	F
See list in text.	BG-Between Groups WG-Within Groups			*Sig. at .05 **Sig. at .01
75.	BG	.9643	1.0	
	WG	15.7143	26.0	
	Total	16.6786	27.0	1.5955
76.	BG	5.2500	1.0	
	WG	6.0000	26.0	
	Total	11.2500	27.0	22.7500**
77.	BG	7.4312	1.0	
	WG	9.3095	25.0	
	Total	16.7407	26.0	19.9560**
78.	BG	.0026	1.0	
	WG	3.4048	25.0	
	Total	3.4074	26.0	.0194
79.	BG	3.8571	1.0	
	WG	8.5714	26.0	
	Total	12.4286	27.0	11.7000**
80.	BG	1.7143	1.0	
	WG	8.0000	26.0	
	Total	9.7143	27.0	5.5714*

Constant V: Median Years of Education for Male Negroes

Variables	Sum of Squares		Degrees of Freedom	F
1.	BG	.0476	1.0	
	WG	3.8095	26.0	
	Total	3.8571	27.0	.3250
2.	BG	2.0119	1.0	
	WG	53.2381	26.0	
	Total	55.2500	27.0	.9826
3.	BG	6.2976	1.0	
	WG	20.6667	26.0	
	Total	26.9643	27.0	7.9228**
4.	BG	15.4286	1.0	
	WG	3.4286	26.0	
	Total	18.8571	27.0	117.0000**

Variables	Sum of Squares		Degrees of Freedom	F
See list in text.	BG-Between Groups WG-Within Groups			*Sig. at .05 **Sig. at .01
5.	BG	15.2381	1.0	
	WG	3.4286	25.0	
	Total	18.6667	26.0	111.1111**
6.	BG	6.2976	1.0	
	WG	44.3810	26.0	
	Total	50.6786	27.0	3.6893
7.	BG	3.0087	1.0	
	WG	10.3759	24.0	
	Total	13.3846	25.0	6.9592*
8.	BG	1.6615	1.0	
	WG	20.8000	24.0	
	Total	22.4615	25.0	1.9172
9.	BG	.3556	1.0	
	WG	16.4444	18.0	
	Total	16.8000	19.0	.3892
10.	BG	.0804	1.0	
	WG	20.3571	14.0	
	Total	20.4375	15.0	.0553
11.	BG	.8308	1.0	
	WG	8.7692	13.0	
	Total	9.6000	14.0	1.2316
12.	BG	.2238	1.0	
	WG	4.5455	11.0	
	Total	4.7692	12.0	.5415
13. Constant	-	-	-	
	-	-	-	
	-	-	-	-
14.	BG	3.3247	1.0	
	WG	24.8571	9.0	
	Total	28.1818	10.0	1.2038
15.	BG	3.0000	1.0	
	WG	45.0000	14.0	
	Total	48.0000	15.0	.9333

Variables		Sum of Squares	Degrees of Freedom	F
See list in text.	BG-Between Groups WG-Within Groups			*Sig. at .05 **Sig. at .01
16.	BG	1.3000	1.0	
	WG	3.2000	16.0	
	Total	4.5000	17.0	6.5000*
17.	BG	.1263	1.0	
	WG	2.4000	17.0	
	Total	2.5263	18.0	.8947
18.	BG	.9643	1.0	
	WG	5.1429	26.0	
	Total	6.1071	27.0	4.8750*
19.	BG	3.0476	1.0	
	WG	29.8095	26.0	
	Total	32.8571	27.0	
20.	BG	9.3333	1.0	
	WG	11.5238	26.0	
	Total	20.8571	27.0	21.0579**
21.	BG	6.8571	1.0	
	WG	20.5714	26.0	
	Total	27.4286	27.0	8.6667**
22.	BG	.0682	1.0	
	WG	19.7500	20.0	
	Total	19.8182	21.0	.0690
23.	BG	2.0720	1.0	
	WG	5.7375	19.0	
	Total	7.8095	20.0	6.8616*
24.	BG	1.9445	1.0	
	WG	21.5940	24.0	
	Total	23.5385	25.0	2.1611
25.	BG	.4399	1.0	
	WG	16.0602	24.0	
	Total	16.5000	25.0	.6573
26.	BG	.0035	1.0	
	WG	16.8661	21.0	
	Total	16.8696	22.0	.0043

Variables	Sum of Squares		Degrees of Freedom	F
See list in text.	BG-Between Groups WG-Within Groups			*Sig. at .05 **Sig. at .01
27.	BG	.7622	1.0	
	WG	8.2778	23.0	
	Total	9.0400	24.0	2.1179
28.	BG	.1029	1.0	
	WG	24.8571	23.0	
	Total	24.9600	24.0	.0952
29.	BG	.0714	1.0	
	WG	15.9286	23.0	
	Total	16.0000	24.0	.1031
30.	BG	.0018	1.0	
	WG	7.6905	11.0	
	Total	7.6923	12.0	.0026
31.	BG	.2961	1.0	
	WG	18.1654	24.0	
	Total	18.4615	25.0	.3912
32.	BG	.2381	1.0	
	WG	18.4286	25.0	
	Total	18.6667	26.0	.3230
33.	BG	.9643	1.0	
	WG	17.7143	26.0	
	Total	18.6786	27.0	1.4153
34.	BG	.4286	1.0	
	WG	18.5714	26.0	
	Total	19.0000	27.0	.6000
35.	BG	.0119	1.0	
	WG	11.2381	26.0	
	Total	11.2500	27.0	.0275
36.	BG	.1905	1.0	
	WG	9.5238	26.0	
	Total	9.7143	27.0	.5200
37.	BG	.1071	1.0	
	WG	20.8571	26.0	
	Total	20.9643	27.0	.1336

Variables	Sum of Squares		Degrees of Freedom	F
See list in text.	BG-Between Groups WG-Within Groups			*Sig. at .05 **Sig. at .01
38.	BG	.9470	1.0	
	WG	20.3864	13.0	
	Total	21.3333	14.0	.6039
39.	BG	1.1905	1.0	
	WG	21.2381	26.0	
	Total	22.4286	27.0	
40.	BG	1.0000	1.0	
	WG	19.5000	16.0	
	Total	20.5000	17.0	.8205
41.	BG	1.9566	1.0	
	WG	11.2286	25.0	
	Total	13.1852	26.0	4.3563*
42.	BG	3.1431	1.0	
	WG	22.2643	25.0	
	Total	25.4074	26.0	3.5293
43.	BG	.7619	1.0	
	WG	24.6667	26.0	
	Total	25.4286	27.0	.8031
44.	BG	2.0119	1.0	
	WG	22.0952	26.0	
	Total	24.1071	27.0	2.3675
45.	BG	.7619	1.0	
	WG	16.0952	26.0	
	Total	16.8571	27.0	1.2308
46.	BG	.8595	1.0	
	WG	19.8071	25.0	
	Total	20.6667	26.0	1.0849
47.	BG	2.0119	1.0	
	WG	21.2381	26.0	
	Total	23.2500	27.0	2.4630
48.	BG	.1905	1.0	
	WG	7.2381	26.0	
	Total	7.4286	27.0	.6842

Variables	Sum of Squares		Degrees of Freedom	F
See list in text.	BG-Between Groups WG-Within Groups			*Sig. at .05 **Sig. at .01
49.	BG	5.7619	1.0	
	WG	11.2381	26.0	
	Total	17.0000	27.0	
50.	BG	.7576	1.0	
	WG	6.3333	20.0	
	Total	7.0909	21.0	2.3923
51.	BG	.0013	1.0	
	WG	16.1587	23.0	
	Total	16.1600	24.0	.0018
52.	BG	1.7143	1.0	
	WG	5.7143	26.0	
	Total	7.4286	27.0	7.8000**
53.	BG	.0086	1.0	
	WG	13.9143	25.0	
	Total	14.0000	26.0	.1540
54.	BG	3.0476	1.0	
	WG	19.8095	26.0	
	Total	22.8571	27.0	4.0000
55.	BG	.0476	1.0	
	WG	21.8095	26.0	
	Total	21.8571	27.0	.0568
56.	BG	.1905	1.0	
	WG	10.6667	26.0	
	Total	10.8571	27.0	.4643
57.	BG	.0119	1.0	
	WG	4.6667	26.0	
	Total	4.6786	27.0	.0663
58.	BG	2.6987	1.0	
	WG	20.2643	25.0	
	Total	22.9630	26.0	3.3294
59.	BG	.4667	1.0	
	WG	10.2000	25.0	
	Total	10.6667	26.0	1.1438

Variables	Sum of Squares		Degrees of Freedom	F
See list in text.	BG-Between Groups WG-Within Groups			*Sig. at .05 **Sig. at .01
60.	BG	.9643	1.0	
	WG	20.2857	26.0	
	Total	21.2500	27.0	1.2359
61.	BG	.1905	1.0	
	WG	26.6667	26.0	
	Total	26.8571	27.0	.1857
62.	BG	.9646	1.0	
	WG	3.7143	26.0	
	Total	4.6786	27.0	6.7500*
63.	BG	1.5696	1.0	
	WG	11.3000	21.0	
	Total	12.8696	22.0	2.9169
64.	BG	.1071	1.0	
	WG	14.5714	26.0	
	Total	14.6786	27.0	.1912
65.	BG	.2709	1.0	
	WG	18.9143	25.0	
	Total	19.1852	26.0	.3581
66.	BG	.0119	1.0	
	WG	20.6667	26.0	
	Total	20.6786	27.0	.0150
67.	BG	.0476	1.0	
	WG	20.6667	26.0	
	Total	20.7143	27.0	.0599
68.	BG	.4286	1.0	
	WG	20.0000	26.0	
	Total	20.4286	27.0	.5571
69.	BG	1.3762	1.0	
	WG	48.4333	19.0	
	Total	49.8095	20.0	
70.	BG	.5833	1.0	
	WG	47.5238	26.0	
	Total	48.1071	27.0	.3191

Variables		Sum of Squares	Degrees of Freedom	F
See list in text.	BG-Between Groups WG-Within Groups			*Sig. at .05 **Sig. at .01
71.	BG	.5833	1.0	
	WG	20.0952	26.0	
	Total	20.6786	27.0	.7547
72.	BG	.4286	1.0	
	WG	28.2857	26.0	
	Total	28.7143	27.0	.3939
73.	BG	.0476	1.0	
	WG	8.6667	26.0	
	Total	8.7143	27.0	.1429
74.	BG	6.8809	1.0	
	WG	9.7857	25.0	
	Total	16.6667	26.0	17.5791**
75.	BG	.9643	1.0	
	WG	11.7143	26.0	
	Total	12.6786	27.0	2.1402
76.	BG	3.4405	1.0	
	WG	9.2381	26.0	
	Total	12.6786	27.0	9.6830**
77.	BG	7.4312	1.0	
	WG	7.3095	25.0	
	Total	14.7407	26.0	25.4162**
78.	BG	.0026	1.0	
	WG	4.0714	25.0	
	Total	44.0740	26.0	.0162
79.	BG	3.4405	1.0	
	WG	9.2381	26.0	
	Total	12.6786	27.0	9.6830**
80.	BG	1.4405	1.0	
	WG	8.6667	26.0	
	Total	10.1071	27.0	4.3214*

APPENDIX D

PERTINENT VARIABLES -- TOTAL 23 x 23 CORRELATION MATRIX

Row/Column	1	2	3	4	5	6	7	8	9	10
1	.26									
2										
3										
4		.48								
5		.36		.36						
6					.26					
7										
8										
9				-.23						
10		.29			.26					
11	.27							.30		
12								.25		
13	.31							.25		
14	.28									.25
15										
16										
17								.24		
18							.25	.34		
19										
20										
21										
22	-.24	.24								
23										

PERTINENT VARIABLES -- TOTAL 23 x 23 CORRELATION MATRIX

Row/Column	11	12	13	14	15	16	17	18	19	20
11										
12										
13		.63								
14		.31	.31							
15			.33	.30						
16	.24		.29							
17	.28	.38	.28							
18			.34				.27			
19										
20									.30	
21									.36	.45
22									.24	.53
23										.43

Row/Column	21	22	23
21			
22	.47		
23	.38	.48	

TESTED VARIABLES -- COMPLETE 80 x 80 CORRELATION MATRIX

Row/Column	1	2	3	4	5	6	7	8	9	10
1										
2										
3										
4			.80							
5										
6					.35					
7						.57				
8							.24			
9		.26						.23		
10									.58	
11								.24	.55	.45
12								.25	.34	.45
13									.32	.35
14		.25							.37	.35
15									.30	
16									.41	.29
17					-.32					
18					-.28	-.24		.24		
19			.30	.37	.51	.27				
20					.64	.34				
21					.37					
22										

TESTED VARIABLES -- COMPLETE 80 x 80 CORRELATION MATRIX

Row/Column	1	2	3	4	5	6	7	8	9	10
23					.41	.30				
24										
25										
26										
27										
28										
29										
30										
31										
32										
33										
34										
35										
36					.32					
37										
38					-.41	-.26				
39					.24					
40										
41					.28					
42		.29								
43							.24			
44										

TESTED VARIABLES -- COMPLETE 80 x 80 CORRELATION MATRIX

Row/Column	1	2	3	4	5	6	7	8	9	10
45		.31								
46										
47										
48		.27								
49										
50										
51										
52										
53										
54										
55										
56										
57										
58										
59										
60						.27				
61						.38				
62						-.27				
63										
64						.23				
65										
66										

TESTED VARIABLES -- COMPLETE 80 x 80 CORRELATION MATRIX

Row/Column	1	2	3	4	5	6	7	8	9	10
67										
68										
69						.24				
70						.23				
71										
72						.32				
73										
74				.26						
75				.26						
76			.39	.39		.28				
77			.26	.33		.38				
78						.23				
79		-.27	.37	.42		.35				
80			.27	.25		.28				

Row/Column	11	12	13	14	15	16	17	18	19	20
11										
12	.63									
13	.43	.48								
14	.37	.27	.47							
15	.24			.33						
16	.36	.23		.37	.58					

TESTED VARIABLES -- COMPLETE 80 x 80 CORRELATION MATRIX

Row/Column	11	12	13	14	15	16	17	18	19	20
17										
18					.25	.26	.57			
19										
20									.42	
21									.39	.38
22										
23							-.27		.41	.43
24										
25										
26										
27										
28										
29										.24
30										
31										
32										
33										
34										
35										
36										.27
37		.23								
38	.30	.27							-.25	-.28

TESTED VARIABLES -- COMPLETE 80 x 80 CORRELATION MATRIX

Row/Column	11	12	13	14	15	16	17	18	19	20
39									.24	
40										-.27
41										
42							.29	.31		
43										
44										
45										
46										
47										
48										
49										
50										
51									.37	.28
52										
53										
54										
55										.23
56										
57										
58	.24	.25								
59										
60									.28	

TESTED VARIABLES -- COMPLETE 80 x 80 CORRELATION MATRIX

Row/Column	11	12	13	14	15	16	17	18	19	20
61									.33	
62										
63										
64		.25								
65										
66							.34	.23		
67										.35
68										
69									.35	.38
70									.37	.39
71										
72									.29	.31
73										
74										
75										
76										
77										
78										
79									.25	
80										

TESTED VARIABLES -- COMPLETE 80 x 80 CORRELATION MATRIX

Row/Column	21	22	23	24	25	26	27	28	29	30
21										
22	.28									
23										
24										
25				.31						
26										
27				.34						
28										
29			.26					.37		
30								.29		
31								.25		.32
32										.37
33								.27		.38
34					.27					
35										
36										
37										.27
38			-.23							
39										
40					.23					
41	.26									
42										.25

TESTED VARIABLES -- COMPLETE 80 x 80 CORRELATION MATRIX

Row/Column	21	22	23	24	25	26	27	28	29	30
43										
44										.24
45										
46										
47										
48				.24						
49		.49								
50										
51										
52										.26
53							.27			.25
54								.30		
55										
56										
57							.29			
58										
59										
60	.27									
61										
62							.26			
63										.39
64			.30					.24		

TESTED VARIABLES -- COMPLETE 80 x 80 CORRELATION MATRIX

Row/Column	21	22	23	24	25	26	27	28	29	30
65										.36
66										
67	.26		.27							
68								.24		.25
69			.30							.38
70	.25		.24					.29	.27	.36
71										.31
72			.37							.33
73	.23									.30
74										
75										
76										
77										
78			.23							
79										
80										

Row/Column	31	32	33	34	35	36	37	38	39	40
31										
32	.34									
33	.29	.48								
34										

TESTED VARIABLES -- COMPLETE 80 x 80 CORRELATION MATRIX

Row/Column	31	32	33	34	35	36	37	38	39	40
35		.33	.27							
36										
37	.37									
38										
39										
40			.24					.27		
41										
42	.33	.26	.39				.30			
43	.31	.28	.29				.26			
44	.28	.26	.27					.24		
45	.39	.26	.36				.27	.23		
46										
47										
48	.31	.34								
49										
50	.24	.35			.40	.27				
51										
52		.43	.28		.27					
53										
54	.28									
55										
56			.25							

TESTED VARIABLES -- COMPLETE 80 x 80 CORRELATION MATRIX

Row/Column	31	32	33	34	35	36	37	38	39	40
57										
58										
59										
60										
61						.26				
62								.25		
63	.37	.39	.25				.30			
64		.29								
65	.33	.42	.43				.24			
66		.34	.39							
67						.25				
68	.26	.24	.28				.36			
69	.26	.32			.28					
70	.28	.32			.25	.26	.27			
71	.33	.33	.26							
72										
73	.28	.30	.28		.26					
74										
75										
76										
77										
78										

TESTED VARIABLES -- COMPLETE 80 x 80 CORRELATION MATRIX

Row/Column	31	32	33	34	35	36	37	38	39	40
79										
80										

Row/Column	41	42	43	44	45	46	47	48	49	50
41										
42										
43		.64								
44		.43	.57							
45		.65	.64	.63						
46										
47		.23	.29		.25					
48	.24		.32	.45	.32					
49										
50								.25		
51										
52								.25		.29
53					.25					
54	.28	.24	.25	.25				.33		
55										
56		.31	.24							
57				.30	.32			.29		
58										

TESTED VARIABLES -- COMPLETE 80 x 80 CORRELATION MATRIX

Row/Column	41	42	43	44	45	46	47	48	49	50
59								.23		
60										
61						.25				
62		.24		.24	.27					
63		.26	.32	.31	.23			.32	.23	.24
64								.26		
65		.29	.38	.27	.28					
66		.40	.41	.36	.44			.31		.28
67										.24
68					.36			.24		
69										.24
70										.27
71		.26	.31							
72										.26
73				.24					.25	
74										
75										
76										
77										
78										
79										
80										

TESTED VARIABLES -- COMPLETE 80 x 80 CORRELATION MATRIX

Row/Column	51	52	53	54	55	56	57	58	59	60
51										
52										
53										
54										
55										
56					.27					
57						.23				
58			.30							
59										
60										
61										.23
62									.26	
63										
64		.35		.26						
65										
66		.26			.23		.27			
67										
68										
69	.33	.41		.28						.28
70	.31	.37		.26						.24
71		.37			.24	.23				
72		.24								

TESTED VARIABLES -- COMPLETE 80 x 80 CORRELATION MATRIX

Row/Column	51	52	53	54	55	56	57	58	59	60
73		.31								
74	.31									
75	.24									
76										
77										
78										
79	.26									
80										

Row/Column	61	62	63	64	65	66	67	68	69	70
61										
62										
63										
64			.29							
65			.54							
66		.23			.28					
67			.25							
68			.26		.27					
69				.35				.30		
70			.25	.36				.40	.74	.24
71			.25	.31	.31				.38	.35
72	.24			.29					.44	

TESTED VARIABLES -- COMPLETE 80 x 80 CORRELATION MATRIX

Row/Column	61	62	63	64	65	66	67	68	69	70
73			.28		.35					.28
74										
75										
76										
77	.25									
78										
79	.28									
80										

Row/Column	71	72	73	74	75	76	77	78	79	80
71										
72	.38									
73										
74										
75										
76				.29	.41					
77		.27		.37	.46	.43				
78							.36			
79					.68	.53	.45			
80						.43	.36	.40	.48	

APPENDIX E

METROPOLITAN BOARD OF EDUCATION
2601 BRANSFORD AVENUE
NASHVILLE, TENNESSEE 37204

July 31, 1964
(Dictated July 30, 1964)

Mr. Sheldon Stoff
School of Education
Cornell University
Ithaca, New York

Dear Mr. Stoff:

This is in reply to your letter of July 27. I am of the opinion that the presence of police in plain clothes and the employment of Negroes on the police force during the period of school desegregation, in which period we still are, as a matter of fact, did not in any way contribute to racial unrest. I am further of the opinion that our use of police in plain clothes was very helpful and that the employment of Negroes on the police force was and still is a very wise thing. It is very important that all officers be wisely assigned. This is true of both white and Negro officers and it is true both of those who are in uniform and those who wear plain clothes.

Do not hesitate to ask me further questions if you have occasion to do so.

Yours very truly,

Wm. Henry Oliver
Co-Superintendent

WHO:mm

P.S. It is my opinion that the local Police Department has saved the Nashville School System twice. I mean that on two occasions the Police Department enabled us to keep all schools open when otherwise some or possibly all of them would have had to close. In 1957, our Police Department saved us from extremist segregationists. During the 1963-64 school year, it saved us from extremist integrationists. It would be difficult to exaggerate in speaking of the debt which public education in our community owes to the local Police Department.

INDEX

T

U

V

W